THE PROPOSED HAWAII INTER-ISLAND SEA FERRY SYSTEM

Feasibility and Its Probable Impact on the Hawaiian Economy

by

Economic Research Center
University of Hawaii
Honolulu, Hawaii

March, 1965

THE PROPOSED HAWAII INTER-ISLAND SEA FERRY SYSTEM
Feasibility and Its Probable Impact on the Hawaiian Economy

by

William A. Dymsza
Visiting Professor of Business Economics,
University of Hawaii, 1964-1965.
Associate Professor of Business Administration,
School of Business, Rutgers-The State University

Fred C. Hung
Associate Professor of Economics,
Acting Director, Economic Research Center,
University of Hawaii

Chris A. Theodore
Visiting Associate Professor of Statistics,
University of Hawaii, 1964-1965.
Associate Professor of Business Administration,
Boston University

with consulting services of

James C. Byrnes
Director, Operating Analysis Division,
Federal Home Loan Bank Board

Charles F. Heye
Assistant Professor of Management,
Coordinator, Small Business Management Program,
University of Hawaii

Economic Research Center
University of Hawaii
Honolulu, Hawaii

March, 1965

ECONOMIC RESEARCH CENTER PUBLICATIONS POLICY

The Economic Research Center was established as an integral part of the University of Hawaii by Act 150 of the 1959 Legislative Session. Its functions, as prescribed by law, are:

"1. To evaluate and secure evidence on the economic effects of proposed and enacted legislation.

2. To perform basic economic research necessary for the operations of various government agencies.

3. To perform continuing economic and statistical research for the welfare of the community as a whole.

4. To evaluate the effects of national legislation and national and international developments on the economy of Hawaii.

5. To promote understanding of our economy."

As a university research agency, the Economic Research Center seeks to perform these functions in an entirely objective manner. This means the approach in each case must be from the viewpoint of the general welfare and not from that of any social, economic, or political interest group.

Each research study is carried out under the direction of a person judged to be professionally competent according to usual academic standards. In keeping with the tenets of academic freedom, the Economic Research Center encourages the full and free development of views on the part of its research personnel, subject to the broad constraint of maintaining scientific objectivity. Such a policy means that any opinions expressed are those of the authors alone and do not necessarily represent the views of the University of Hawaii nor any of its administrative or academic subdivisions.

Preface

This study was requested by the State Legislature (Senate Concurrent Resolution No. 26, Budget Session of 1964) and financed by the State Department of Transportation. It represents an attempt to take a new look at the long-debated ferry issue and to provide basic information upon which the legislators and state officials can make intelligent decisions. As we have emphasized in this report, it is not our intention to give an answer to the question as to whether there should or should not be a ferry. Instead, we have examined the facts and on the basis of our research and professional judgment we present the pros and cons of the situation. Whether a particular legislator or state official decides for or against the proposed ferry depends on the weight he might assign to the findings of this study as well as to other considerations.

Because of the large number of ifs and buts contained in the findings, we have deliberately avoided giving a summary and conclusions chapter. The readers are asked to read the whole report. In case they are short of time, they are advised to read at least Chapters II, III, IV, V, VI, VII, and VIII.

This report has truly been the joint effort of the three authors, with significant contributions from the two consultants, Mr. James Byrnes and Professor Charles Heye.

The staff of the Economic Research Center worked hard in getting this report in published form. Special thanks are due to Mrs. Angeles Ortiz and Mr. William Wan for their research assistance; to Mrs. Sarah Wang, Mrs. Karen Higa, and Miss Coral Hack for their proofreading; and to Misses Joyce Takabayashi, Audrey Endo, Dale Fujimoto, Stella Daida, and Mrs. Shanta Pandey and others for their typing and clerical help. Without this wonderful help, this report will never see the light of the day.

We would also like to thank Dr. Wytze Gorter and Dr. Robert Kamins for kindly reviewing most of the chapters.

Needless to say, the authors assume the full responsibility for any errors which might still remain in this report.

William A. Dymsza

Fred C. Hung

Chris A. Theodore

TABLE OF CONTENTS

LIST OF TABLES

LIST OF TABLES

viii

PART ONE

INTRODUCTION

Since 1955, when Captain Richardson advanced the idea for the first time,

there have been numerous proposals and studies for an inter-island ferry in the

State of Hawaii. A bibliography on the subject is appended to this chapter. It

may be of interest to know that the cost of these studies exceeds a quarter of

a million dollars. This sum does not include the cost of the present study (not

to exceed $34,000) nor the cost of a few earlier studies and proposals which did

not involve an out-of-pocket expenditure.

With the time and effort already spent on the subject the reader of this

report may immediately raise a number of pertinent questions: Why another study?

Isn't the information and advice contained in the earlier studies sufficient for

a decision? What are the reasons which may justify a new look at an old and

seemingly well-covered subject? The reader will be able to find answers to

questions such as these in the material contained in Part One of our report.

Chapter I briefly reviews and evaluates certain aspects of the earlier studies on

the subject. Chapter II sets out directives for research, defines the scope, and

explains the methodology of this report.

CHAPTER I

A BRIEF REVIEW AND EVALUATION OF EARLIER PROPOSALS AND STUDIES

The existing reports on an inter-island ferry vary a great deal in several respects but especially with respect to the definition of the problem and its scope, the concept of a ferry and its technical aspects, the demand for such a service, and the conclusions reached. Thus, no attempt has been made to summarize their content. Instead, our main objective in this chapter is to discuss and analyze the description of the proposed inter-island ferries, estimates of the demand for such a service, and cost estimates. Such a treatment will establish the necessary conceptual continuity with past efforts and ideas. More important than that, however, it will give us the opportunity to evaluate from the methodological standpoint earlier findings and conclusions. This evaluation will enable us to give our research effort purpose and direction.

1. Description of Proposed Ferries

Early proposals.--The first proposal for an inter-island ferry service that attracted widespread attention was by Captain Gill Richardson, USN, in a feature article appearing in The Honolulu Advertiser in December, 1955. Captain Richardson proposed a luxury, one-ship ferry service between the islands offering three round trips per week to each of the major ports. The ship was to be a luxury vessel with a speed of 20 knots and a capacity of 600 passengers and 125 automobiles. Some of the luxury aspects of the service were a cafeteria capable of seating 200 persons, a bar, a card room, a barber shop, a beauty shop, and 20 staterooms. Roll-on, roll-off operations for passenger cars and trucks were proposed, with minimum turn-around time at major ports.

The two reports by John B. Ward Associates in March, 1956 and June, 1956 mainly evaluated the luxury type one-ship ferry proposed by Captain Richardson and concluded that such an operation would involve substantial losses. The reports also focused attention on an alternative--an economy type ferry ship serving the islands. As a result of their analysis, the Ward reports suggested a point-to-point shuttle type of ferry system, involving smaller ships and shorter trips between the closest points in the islands. They suggested that such a ferry system be installed on a step-by-step basis.

The John Child & Co. report primarily concentrated on a market analysis of demand for inter-island sea travel and failed to deal with a description of such a service. It did not deal with the mode of transport, type and frequency of service, the routes and other aspects. It did suggest average rates of $25 for a family group and $30 for a car on a trip to another island, based upon average transportation costs of a vacation by a family group for an automobile trip of 100 miles or more on the mainland. As we shall emphasize later, a major weakness of the demand estimates was that they were not related to a definite, clearly defined ferry service.

Law and Wilson-Tudor report.--By far the most comprehensive report undertaken on the physical aspects of an inter-island ferry service was the Law and Wilson-Tudor report entitled, "The State of Hawaii Transportation Plan."

This report covered most aspects of land, air, and water transportation in Hawaii, with particular emphasis on the need for inter-island ferry transportation. The ferry section of the report tried to determine the best way of meeting the needs for convenient, frequent, low cost, "mass" transportation service for persons traveling with their cars. The study also tried to determine how to provide improved inter-island freight service for business firms.

After considering the requirements of a ferry system to handle passengers and cargo, the comfort of passengers, seasonal characteristics, the need for dependability, speed, and frequency of service, alternative types of ships and routes, and other factors, the study recommended a "Preferred Water Ferry Plan" based on two identical ships in a long-haul operation.

The two identical ships would be about 370 feet long and be equipped with fin stabilizers and bow steering in order to assure the passengers a comfortable trip; they would be capable of sustained speeds of about 18 knots. Each ship would have a capacity for carrying 500 passengers and 106 standard-size automobiles or 52 highway trailers. The two ships would cost $12,000,000, and the port and terminal facilities, an additional $7,000,000. As the two ships were identical, they could replace each other when repairs were required.

The ferry service was based primarily on handling passengers and their automobiles, but it also provided for handling some cargo to utilize the capacity of the ships. Cargo was to be handled by rolling on and rolling off trucks and trailers loaded with merchandise.

In order to secure a reasonably comfortable voyage for passengers and shorter trips, the schedule provided for traveling primarily on the leeward side of the islands--going between Honolulu and the ports of Kawaihae on Hawaii, Lahaina on Maui, and Kaunakakai on Molokai. However, in order to serve the requirements of cargo and provide some service to major cities, the ferry would also go to Hilo, Hawaii and Kahului, Maui. In summary, the schedule provided for daily calls at Oahu, Maui and Hawaii and for five trips a week to Kauai and Molokai.

The rates essentially were 60 per cent of airline rates. Provision was made for a family plan. The rate for automobiles was one and one-half times the single passenger rate. As a result of the schedule of rates, a family of four could

take their car with them to another island and return at about the same cost as
the local airline family-plan fare without a car. The rate for cargo was somewhat
above the barge rate, because of faster and more frequent service.

The Law and Wilson-Tudor study based upon comprehensive evaluations of the
engineering and physical aspects of an inter-island ferry service clarified many
aspects of a sea ferry service. It also considered alternatives such as a hydrofoil
service and found that it was not sufficiently proven from the technical standpoint.

However, after determining that the Preferred Water Ferry Plan service would
involve substantial deficits until 1977, based upon calculations of costs and
estimates of demand, the report recommended an air ferry service. The report
proposed a three-plane air ferry with two Argosy 650's, the type of plane flying
the English Channel, capable of handling 20 passengers and two automobiles, and one
Argosy 670, a larger plane to be available in 1964, that could carry six standard
American cars and 30 passengers. It recommended gradually shifting to Argosy 670's.
The rates proposed were basically 10 per cent below existing airline rates for
passengers and somewhat below the existing barge rate for automobiles.

The reasons for recommending the air ferry system were that (a) it would
involve smaller capital investments in aircraft and terminal and port facilities
than the sea ferry; (b) in part because of smaller capital investments the subsidies
would be considerably smaller; (c) the air ferry would be more flexible in adjusting
schedules to demand and in adapting to handling passengers, automobiles and cargo;
(d) in case of need, it would be easier to dispose of airplanes in second-hand
markets than large ferries; and (e) the operation could be more readily converted
to private ownership, especially by the existing airlines.

However, although it thoroughly discussed the Preferred Water Ferry Plan, the
Law and Wilson-Tudor study probably confused the entire issue by recommending an
air ferry service. As a matter of fact, it failed to analyze the air ferry as

thoroughly as it had the sea ferry service. Also in recommending the air ferry it abandoned the concept of a low-cost, "mass" transportation service for persons traveling with their cars to other islands. The air ferry service as proposed could not be a method of low-cost, mass travel for persons with their cars. An air ferry would especially have difficulty in handling large numbers of cars. It could not provide adequate service during the peak periods of travel, according to the demand estimates used in their study. In order to handle peak periods of traffic, there would have to be an increase in the number of planes; this would increase investment costs substantially. Also, under the rates proposed as well as the service provided, the system would hardly be likely to encourage a major increase in inter-island travel. Experience shows that where air ferries are used to transport cars and passengers as in the English Channel, they are a supplementary service to a sea ferry.

Nevertheless, any study of an inter-island ferry service has to consider carefully the basic aspects of the Preferred Water Ferry Plan elaborated in the Law and Wilson-Tudor report. The study placed major emphasis on a sea ferry service primarily transporting passengers with their automobiles. Also, after evaluating different types of vessels and routes and considering the comfort of passengers, it recommended two ocean-going ships about 370 feet long with fin stabilizers and an average speed of 18 knots. It also suggested going primarily to ports on the leeward side of the island where the seas are not as rough and the distances involved are shorter. However, the study also recommended that a ferry go to Hilo and Kahului, the commercial centers of the islands of Hawaii and Maui, in order to provide better service for cargo.

But in several ways the study was not able to reconcile the requirements of passengers and cargo. It seemed to feel that passengers with their automobiles would use most of the capacity of the ferries during the peak summer periods and

then there would be considerable capacity for cargo in the non-peak periods. Yet, the peak periods in cargo in some cases would occur at the same time as the peak periods in carrying passengers. Furthermore, shippers of cargo would have to be assured of year-round service. It would not be enough to provide cargo service if the ferry boats had available space. Furthermore, cargo on ferries was to be handled by a roll-on, roll-off operation of trucks and trailers. No adequate study was made of the feasibility of speedily loading and unloading cargo on such a basis and quick turn-around time consistent with handling passengers. Furthermore, as we shall emphasize later, there was no adequate study whether businessmen would or could use that type of cargo service.

The Hulten Proposal.--During the 1961 legislative session, Senator John Hulten submitted two statements in support of the operation of a sea ferry service by the state. These statements were based upon Mr. Hulten's investigations and consultations with various maritime experts and some surveys conducted. These statements found an air ferry service to be completely inadequate. In essence they favored a two-ship ferry system along the lines suggested by the Preferred Water Ferry Plan of the Law and Wilson-Tudor report. The major differences were that Mr. Hulten stated that minimum rates were necessary to encourage mass inter-island travel; he actually suggested ferry rates about 30 per cent of existing airline rates. Also, his report emphasized cargo as highly important in using the capacity of the ferry, but the problem was not analyzed thoroughly. Finally, he felt that state operation of the ferry was essential in order to have minimum rates.

Parsons, Brinckerhoff, Quade & Douglas Report.--This report considered both a water and air ferry service. For a water ferry it suggested some revisions of the Preferred Water Ferry Plan of the Law and Wilson-Tudor report. It recommended

two ships, one a modern ocean-going vessel with a speed of 23.5 knots capable of handling 600 passengers and 150 automobiles and the other a smaller ship, 365 feet long, with a speed of 16 knots and capable of carrying 400 passengers and 130 automobiles or in place of the second ship a converted used ship such as the "City of Havana." The larger and speedier ship would operate daily on the leeward side between Honolulu and Kawaihae, Hawaii, with intermediate stops on alternative days at Maui and Molokai. Its speed, approximating that of the fast, modern European ferries would enable it to complete its daily trip within a 16-hour working day. This ship would take care of most of the passengers with their automobiles going between Oahu, Maui, Molokai and Hawaii. The second ship, either the smaller ship or a converted used ship, would make round trips between Honolulu and Kauai three times a week and round trips between Honolulu and Kahului (Maui) and Hilo twice a week. This ship would take care of passengers, cars and cargo between Oahu and Kauai and that going to Hilo and north Maui. Unlike the Law and Wilson-Tudor report, the two ferry ships would not be interchangeable and could not directly replace each other.

Since the study was not certain that there was adequate demand for a sea ferry service or that its own demand estimates were realistic, it recommended that a ferry system be initiated on a trial basis, preferably for a period of 18 months by leasing the equipment. It recognized that it was difficult to lease a ship for a sea ferry service.

The report examined an air ferry service. After considering different types of aircraft available, it determined that the most suitable aircraft for an air ferry service was an ATC "Carvair," a modified DC-4. It recommended that a test run be undertaken between Honolulu and Kamuela, Hawaii, for a period of 18 months to determine if people would travel with their cars to other islands. This test run would be undertaken by leasing one Carvair plane from an air leasing agency

for a period of 18 months. The report suggested five round trips or possibly six round trips per day from Honolulu to Hilo. If demand exceeded capacity, a second plane could be added.

The report recognized that the air ferry service proposed would be inadequate to meet its projected estimates of demand. It would be especially inadequate to meet demand during peak travel periods. The report also recognized that an air ferry service was not a way of providing adequate transportation for large numbers of people with their cars over the long term. In order to handle large numbers of people with cars, there would have to be a substantial investment in airplanes. This becomes a costly operation especially for handling cars. The report indicated that if a trial air ferry service was highly successful, the state might find that it would have to set up a sea ferry service.

In many ways, the Parsons, Brinckerhoff, Quade & Douglas report did more to confuse than clarify the problem. Its proposal to have two different type ships, one a larger ocean-going vessel with a speed of 23½ knots and the other a smaller vessel with a speed of 16 knots, was in many respects inferior to the Law and Wilson-Tudor report. The ships could not be interchanged to assure continuation of a fairly adequate service, when one of the vessels was being repaired. There are economies involved through interchangeability of spare parts and in other ways in having two identical ships. Also, the advantage of having a larger, speedier ship on the run from Honolulu to Kawaihae, including less-frequent stops on Maui and Molokai, was more than offset by having a slow service between Honolulu and Kauai and Hilo. A serious question arises whether many passengers would use such a slow service and how a smaller, slower ship would make out in the rough seas going to Hilo and Kahului. Perhaps, the slower service would be primarily for handling cargo to Hilo and Kahului. But the report failed to analyze in any way the requirements to handle cargo.

Furthermore, the suggestion to try one ship on a lease basis for one year to 18 months was not realistic as appropriate ships were not available. The proposal to lease a "Carvair" plane for a period of 18 months to determine if people would travel with their cars to the other islands could not determine demand for a ferry service. It could only ascertain demand imperfectly for the type of service being offered, considering schedules, rates, and service provided. The air ferry trial proposed could not ascertain demand for a sea ferry. Neither could an air ferry even with two or three planes become a method of low-cost, mass transportation of large numbers of people with their cars. Thus, the report failed to come to grips with some of the major problems involved.

Coverdale and Colpitts report.--The most recent study to examine the problem of a sea ferry in rather comprehensive fashion was the one completed by Coverdale and Colpitts early in 1964. The report recommended a ferry service of two ships-- one similar to that described in the Law and Wilson-Tudor report, a 370-foot ocean-going vessel with a speed of 18 knots with fin stabilizers and a capacity of 500 passengers and 106 standard automobiles and the other a converted used ship, such as the Empire State II, with a length of 424 feet, fin stabilizers, speed of 16½ knots and a capacity of about 333 passengers and 82 automobiles. (The Empire State had been recommended as a used ship that could be converted for ferry service in a report by George Sharp in 1963.)

The reason for recommending the new ship and the converted used ship was that the legislature had only authorized $12,000,000 for the acquisition of the ships and for necessary port facilities. This was far from adequate to acquire two new ships and improve the port facilities, as recommended by the Law and Wilson-Tudor report.

11

The Coverdale and Colpitts report recommended that the new ship should make four trips a week between Honolulu and Nawiliwili on Kauai and between Honolulu and Kahului on Maui. The converted used vessel would make four round trips per week mostly during the night time between Honolulu and Hilo. The ports of Kahului on Maui and Hilo on Hawaii were selected because they were the major ports on these islands and were most convenient for passengers and cargo. The report determined that optimum fares for adult passengers were 70 per cent of existing airline rates; the charge for an automobile was twice the rate for an adult passenger, somewhat under existing barge rates.

The report emphasized travel by passengers with automobiles and did not give much attention to handling cargo. It believed that most cargo would be palletized cargo handled by a fork-lift truck operated by the Hawaii State Ferries. It expected that most cargo would be the kind now handled by the airlines. Moreover, it felt that the short turn-around time would not allow much time for handling cargo. It proposed rates equivalent to or somewhat below those charged by the airlines.

The report had some major weaknesses with respect to the description of a sea ferry service. It ignored some of the key recommendations of the Law and Wilson-Tudor report, especially that the sea ferry travel primarily along the leeward side of the island to assure passengers a more comfortable and speedier trip. The ports and routes selected would require travel through rough seas, that might discourage passenger travel. The report did make a definite attempt to stay within a $12,000,000 bond issue approved by the legislature by recommending the purchase and conversion of a used ship to ferry use. However, the use of a converted used ship presented major difficulties. The slow speed of the ship, the long distances involved between Honolulu and Hilo, the rough seas, the inadequate arrangement for passengers, and the trips mostly at night would probably

result in relatively small use of such a service. In fact, the nature of the service might discourage its use, except for cargo and limited passengers. Still, the report failed to adequately consider the matter of a cargo service. The schedule also did not provide for travel between the islands of Maui and Hawaii. Furthermore, the report failed to give reasons why the passenger rates should be 70 per cent of airline rates rather than 60 per cent as recommended in the Law and Wilson-Tudor report. All in all, in many ways the service proposed was considerably inferior to the Preferred Water Ferry Plan in the Law and Wilson-Tudor study.

Guralnick paper.--In a paper presented to the Society of Naval Architects and Marine Engineers in Hawaii in April, 1964, Mr. Morris Guralnick, a naval architect, made some definite suggestions about an inter-island sea ferry service. According to his analysis, the basic need was for a safe, quick, comfortable, inexpensive transportation service for passengers between islands. He felt that service for transportation of cargo was rapidly improving in the islands and did not require major attention in a ferry service. Therefore, a ferry should be primarily designed to carry people with their cars. He listed the following factors as basic in the design of inter-island ferries:

a. Passenger transport with adequate comfort
b. High speed
c. Low fares
d. Minor cargo which will not interfere with passenger schedules
e. Economy of labor and other operating costs
f. Rapid turn around

Mr. Guralnick suggested a design of ships based on simplicity, austerity, utility and functionality. In other words, he suggested an economy ship designed without frills and chrome to provide efficient, reasonably comfortable and speedy transportation for passengers. Along these lines he proposed two identical ships about 300 feet long, with a sustained speed of 20.5 knots, handling approximately 400 passengers and 80 automobiles each. The design of the ship should provide for

driver loading of vehicles under standard conditions and stevedore loadings under special conditions. Since he did not consider cargo important, and in order to reduce costs of construction, he stated that the deck should not be designed to accommodate large trucks or trailers. Essentially, he believed that produce could be transported by the farmers themselves in vehicles hardly larger than standard automobiles. For passengers he recommended comfortable seats with built-in reclining mechanism to permit sleeping, similar to seats used by the airlines.

Instead of fin stabilizers, he suggested the use of flume tanks, because they cost less and are more effective at any speed down to zero. He also recommended an automated restaurant, rather than elaborate commissary facilities. He believed that the type of ship he proposed could be manned by three men--a captain, pilot and engineer--in addition to limited commissary people. He recommended two identical ships, because one could be running while the other was being repaired. He strongly argued against converting a used ship to a ferry service, because it would be inefficient and costly to operate and maintain. He estimated that the cost of each ship would be about $3,300,000 and believed that the ships could be built in Hawaii.

While he recognized that there were several possible routes, he suggested a service involving the two identical ships from Honolulu to Hilo on Hawaii to Kahului on Maui to Kaunakakai on Molokai to Honolulu to Nawiliwili on Kauai and back to Honolulu. Such a trip could be completed in 36 hours, allowing one hour stop-over time at each port. Crews could be shifted similar to practices on airlines. With a lay-over during the middle of the week for minor servicing and repairs, six trips a week could be completed. He suggested going to Hilo and Kahului because these were major ports and principal cities on these islands. However, he did recognize that there could be some changes in routes with some trips going to Kawaihae on Hawaii and Lahaina on Maui.

14

Many aspects of the Guralnick proposal are attractive, but they should be evaluated by competent naval architects. Especially appealing is the ideal of a modern, economy ship without frills with a speed of 20.5 knots at a cost of 3.3 million dollars to transport passengers and automobiles between the islands. Building such ships in Hawaii would be highly appealing to the people in the state.[1] Also attractive are low costs of operation by having a small crew of three and an automatic cafeteria. However, some maritime people expressed doubt whether the ships could be built for 3.3 million dollars, built in Hawaii, and operated with such a small crew.

The Guralnick paper helped to clarify some matters concerning a sea ferry that had been confused by some of the other reports. It emphasized that a sea ferry should be designed primarily to provide passengers with low cost and speedy transportation, rather than to handle cargo. A sea ferry to handle different types of cargo makes the ship more expensive; also the turn-around time makes it difficult for a sea ferry to handle much cargo, except perhaps some produce that can be loaded rapidly. Moreover, rebuilt and converted used ships for ferry service are not appropriate for a modern ferry service, because they are too slow and cumbersome; they are costly to operate; they are not designed for handling ferry passengers and would be expensive to convert to a sea ferry service.

However, the Guralnick proposal is not without problems. The ships recommended by Mr. Guralnick are smaller than those proposed in the Law and Wilson-Tudor study. They might not provide adequate capacity to handle peak traffic or traffic in the long term. Nevertheless, if there were sufficient demand, a third ship could be added. Mr. Guralnick also suggests that the sea ferry go to Hilo on Hawaii and Kahului on Maui through the rough seas. How would the smaller ships he proposes

[1]In a letter to the Economic Research Center dated February 26, 1965, Mr. Guralnick stated that he still believes the ships could be built in Hawaii, although at a somewhat greater cost than 3.3 million dollars.

stand up in these rough seas? Would the voyage be adequately comfortable for passengers on the smaller ships? Mr. Guralnick apparently believes that the ships with flume tanks would provide a reasonably comfortable voyage. Going to Hilo and Kahului means not only rougher seas but also much longer voyages than going on the leeward side to Kawaihae and Maalaea. Since speed is of such importance to passengers how would the longer trips affect passenger travel? Despite the longer voyages and rougher seas, Mr. Guralnick believes that a sea ferry should go to the principal cities in the islands. Here we have a dilemma that is difficult to resolve: should a sea ferry serve the principal cities of the islands or should it select the shortest and smoothest route?

There is a basic problem with an economy ship with no frills. It might have an adverse effect on demand. The ferry rides in Hawaii would be rather long ones, in many cases about five to ten hours. Passengers would expect comfort and adequate restaurant, bar and other facilities. If the voyages were too austere, they might lead to less passenger travel.

Furthermore, while the proposal of a crew of three persons is attractive to keep operating costs down, is it feasible? What would the Coast Guard require? Our talks with Coast Guard officials indicate that such a crew would not be allowed.

As we have seen, there have been widely divergent recommendations with respect to a ferry service, including mode of transport, the type of ships, the routes, the ports served, frequency and other aspects of the service, rates, and emphasis on passengers and cargo. While divergent viewpoints are often wholesome, in the case of a sea ferry they have led to confusion rather than clarification. Some of the differences with respect to the ferry should have been expected for the problem is inherently complex and there are few definitive guide lines based upon past experience. The problem of an adequate ferry system to serve the Hawaiian Islands

has many unique aspects, for which the experiences of most other ferry systems are not very helpful.

2. Estimates of Demand in Previous Studies

The previous studies have encountered major problems in estimating demand for an inter-island ferry service. Various methods have been used to estimate demand, making numerous assumptions, in some cases stated, in other cases not stated. These demand estimates are extremely important for they have been used to determine revenue. We shall briefly consider the methods used to estimate demand and the assumptions made in various studies.

The early studies did not make comprehensive demand estimates and are far out-of-date. Captain Richardson in his proposal to establish a one-ship luxury service did not make a demand estimate. The Ward report, especially the first one, did make a demand estimate for a one-vessel ferry service for one year. But in deriving their demand estimates they made a number of assumptions--some quite arbitrary: that island residents' travel by air indicated potential demand, that tourists would not use a ferry service, and that two-thirds of inter-island pleasure travel and one-third of business travel comprised the potential demand for a ferry service. The basis for making these assumptions was not adequately explained.

John Child & Co. report.--The first comprehensive study of the market for an inter-island sea ferry service was made by the John Child & Co. in 1957. It provided a framework for the demand analysis by discussing the developments and trend of inter-island passenger and freight movements, the available methods of transportation, and some of the changes in technology, production, marketing and the economics of the islands that might affect inter-island transportation.

17

For the first time an attempt was made to make a quantitative estimate of passenger demand for a ferry, considering both island residents and tourists. The study assumed that there was a dormant potential for travel by island residents with their cars to other islands for vacations, comparable to the average rate of vacation travel on the mainland as revealed by a University of Michigan Survey. This survey indicated that the average rate of vacation travel by mainland residents taking trips of 100 miles or more, principally by automobile, was 25.8 per cent-- a rate substantially in excess of that by Hawaiian residents. This was after adjustment for travel by air.

It was also assumed that travel by Hawaiian residents would approximate mainland travel, if transportation and other costs, travel activities and attractions were reasonably equivalent to those on the mainland.

In summary, the procedure of estimating demand was as follows:

a. Potential total demand was determined by using the 25.8 per cent average rate of travel of mainland travel in relation to Hawaiian population.

b. The difference between potential total demand and actual travel was determined and was considered as the amount of additional travel that could be generated.

c. This was converted to a family group basis at 2.5 persons per family.

d. The amount of additional travel was reduced by 50 per cent by considering that families with incomes of less than $5,000 a year would not travel.

e. It was assumed that 70 per cent of vacationing island families would take their autmobiles with them. Finally, on the basis of the average vacation costs on the mainland, the study determined that the average fares should be $25 per family group and $30 per automobile round trip.

18

The study also assumed that 10 per cent of tourists from the mainland would take a trip to a neighboring island, largely because of the novelty, and that 10 per cent of them would ship a car. No empirical basis was provided for this estimate except the experience the John Child & Co. had in working on tourist problems.

The demand estimates have some serious limitations:

a. There is no reason to believe that the average rate of mainland vacation travel, as indicated by a survey of potential total inter-island travel, represents normal travel by Hawaii residents to other islands. Hawaii residents differ in many ways from mainland residents, not only in race, customs, and tastes, but also in their expenditure patterns and discretionary income.

b. Along the same line, the study failed to consider the tendency of some Hawaii residents to travel to the mainland for their vacations.

c. The estimate of demand was not based on any particular type of ferry service. Demand may vary a great deal depending upon the specific service offered, frequency of service, rates, and other aspects.

d. The study considered that travel on a ferry by island residents would be all new or induced travel. It failed to consider that there would be some diversion from air travel to ferry travel. Also, the study did not consider repeat travel.

e. There was no empirical basis for estimating the tourist travel on an inter-island ferry system.

Law and Wilson-Tudor study.--Demand estimates for the Law and Wilson-Tudor report were furnished by the Department of Planning and Research of the State of Hawaii. However, complete details on how these estimates were derived were not provided. The demand estimates considered travel by island residents and tourists based on statistics available on inter-island travel and several sample surveys and in-flight surveys. Demand projections of travel by island residents were

based upon projections of resident population and per capita travel trends. It was assumed that per capita travel of Hawaii residents would increase at about half the rate projected by the Civil Aeronautics Board for the nation as a whole. The demand estimates of inter-island tourist travel were based upon separate projections of out-of-state visitor arrivals and per capita travel trends.

The projections of inter-island travel were initially based upon air passenger rates in constant 1959 dollars. However, the projections were adjusted for various changes in fares. A regression equation was used to determine the elasticity of demand for passenger travel, based upon air travel data available in the 1947-1959 period. The elasticity of demand in the regression equation was used to estimate passenger demand at 60 per cent of air fares. The Department of Planning and Research also made use of a survey of Oahu residents vacationing on neighbor islands in 1959 conducted by the Honolulu Star-Bulletin as part of its annual "Consumer Analysis." An assumption was made that 80 per cent of all surface ferry households would take their cars.

The Law and Wilson-Tudor report had two demand projections of passenger travel for selected years up to 1980, one "with transportation program" and the other "with government program." The government program would include development of public works facilities and government assistance to tourism and other industries to foster maximum economic growth, while the transportation program would only involve improved methods of intra- and inter-island transportation. It was assumed that with only a transportation program passenger travel would be about two-thirds of that with a full government program to promote maximum economic development. While there is no detailed description of projections of cargo movements, the procedures used were comparable to those in ascertaining passenger demand.

The methods used to estimate demand in the Law and Wilson-Tudor report have some serious limitations as indicated below, even considering that complete information was not published about the methods used.

a. The demand estimates of travel by Hawaii residents were based on past travel trends projected into the future on the basis of population projections and per capita travel trends on the mainland. No justification was stated for using one-half of per capita travel trends for Hawaii residents compared to those on the mainland. This assumption limits growth of passenger demand for a ferry service.

b. The demand estimates for inter-island tourist travel were based upon similar types of assumptions concerning numbers of out-of-state visitors and travel trends to the other islands.

c. The elasticity of demand was determined by historical data considering per cent changes in rates and per cent changes in travel in relation to the labor force. It has been found that elasticity of demand calculations for such long historical periods have little validity as there are too many other variables. Moreover, these elasticity calculations were for air travel, and they were used to determine demand for a sea ferry and an air ferry. The elasticity calculations for cargo demand were also based upon historical data over many years and had little relevance because of all kinds of other changes involved.

d. The demand estimates failed to consider shifts or diversions from air travel to a sea ferry or air ferry.

e. No justification was presented for the basis used to estimate that the passenger demand with a transportation program would be about two-thirds of that with a full government program. These ratios were quite arbitrary. Also, there was no justification for the assumption that 80 per cent of the families would take their car with them.

f. The demand estimates for passenger travel were not based upon a definite description of a ferry service. In fact, they were not related in any precise way to the ferry service. They also failed to consider adequately the possibility of Hawaiian residents traveling to other islands with their cars.

g. The projections of demand for an air ferry had similar limitations.

The Craig survey.--In view of criticisms made of the demand estimates in the Law and Wilson-Tudor report, the Department of Planning and Research engaged Robert S. Craig Associates to make a survey of the market for an inter-island ferry system. The Craig study surveyed a random sample of 2,191 households on the major islands of Hawaii by personal interviews with a structured questionnaire. It also surveyed non-random samples of selected businessmen and farmers on shipments on a ferry system, and of tourists staying at some of the major hotels at Waikiki.

The key questions in the survey of households concerned travel to other islands in the preceding 12 months, plans to travel to neighbor islands in the next 12 months, and preferences with respect to travel by existing airlines, a sea ferry, an air ferry, and a hydrofoil ferry. In a general question, the respondents were asked to state their preference with respect to travel by existing air facilities, air ferry, a conventional sea ferry or a hydrofoil craft. Then, in separate questions, the respondents were presented with a description of each ferry service, at specified rates, and were asked to indicate their anticipated travel plans for the next 12 months on the existing airlines or an air ferry, existing airlines or a sea ferry, and existing airlines or a hydrofoil ferry. The survey asked a number of other questions about familiarity with the ferry issue, importance of the issue to people, preferences with respect to travel to neighbor islands and ways of spending vacations, family income, and other matters.

The survey found that there was a considerable amount of inter-island travel by Hawaii residents. About 80 per cent of adult residents had taken trips to other islands sometime or other; about 40 per cent had taken trips to other islands within the past 12 months. About four-fifths of persons who had taken trips to other islands during the past 12 months planned to take additional trips in the near future.

22

Moreover, the survey found that the residents of the state would patronize a new ferry service offering reasonable prices, safety, convenience and comfort. In the general question, there was a somewhat greater preference for the hydrofoil than other types of ferries. Still, when faced with a choice between existing air travel and each of the types of ferries, in separate questions, the highest proportion of respondents preferred (1) the air ferry, (2) the hydrofoil, and (3) the conventional sea ferry. The survey indicated that there would be a substantial increase in people taking their cars with them on a conventional sea ferry or an air ferry. It was inconclusive about whether a new ferry would induce increased inter-island travel, but it found that there would be a considerable diversion from air travel to travel on any of the proposed ferries.

A great deal of other information was obtained in the survey concerning inter-island travel. A higher proportion of people on the neighbor islands than Oahu considered inter-island transportation very important. The costs of transportation, lodging, and food are the major factors that stand in the way of increased inter-island travel. About 70 per cent of the respondents stated that they were willing to see the state provide financial aid to a new ferry system. About six out of ten people, especially Oahu residents, stated that if the state had cabins in state parks, they would be more likely to take vacations on neighbor islands.

The study also surveyed out-of-state visitors staying at 25 Waikiki hotels during the period March 22 through March 29, 1961. A total of 2,272 questionnaires were distributed to 25 of 27 hotels selected at random in Waikiki (two hotels were late in approving distribution of the questionnaires). The questionnaires were completed by hotel guests. About 14 per cent of the total questionnaires distributed (326) were returned by out-of-state visitors (after eliminating residents of Hawaii).

23

In a key question, visitors were asked whether they had visited or planned to visit any of the neighbor islands. They were also asked which mode of travel they would use if given a choice of traveling by existing airlines, air ferry, conventional sea ferry, or hydrofoil ferry. With the questionnaires there was a brief description of the proposed ferries and rates from Honolulu to Kauai. The out-of-state visitors were also asked whether they would be more likely to visit the neighbor islands if it were possible to travel by surface ferry.

About two-thirds of the respondents stated that they had visited or planned to visit one or more of the neighbor islands. When given a choice among travel by existing airlines and by the three types of ferries, a little over one-third stated that they would go by existing air facilities, about one-third by hydrofoil surface ferry, about one-sixth by conventional surface ferry, about one-tenth by air ferry. About one-sixth stated that they did not know or would not go by any mode of transport. In some cases, respondents stated that they would go by more than one mode of travel. Finally, a little over 40 per cent stated that they would be more likely to visit the other islands if it were possible to travel by ferry, while almost as high a percentage stated that they would not be more likely to visit the other islands in such a case; the rest said that they did not know.

The study also surveyed a non-random sample of 305 businessmen and farmers on cargo shipments on the proposed ferries. No specific information is stated on how the specific firms were selected, except that they were expected to be engaged in inter-island shipping. About 380 contacts were made to obtain 305 interviews on the major islands. The distribution of firms by major islands was as follows: Oahu about one-third; Hawaii somewhat over one-quarter; Maui about one-fifth; Kauai about one-seventh, and Molokai about one-twentieth. Almost three-quarters of the respondents were businessmen and the rest were engaged in agricultural activities. After the interviews, it was found that 35 of the respondents did not engage in inter-island shipping, leaving 270 net interviews.

24

The respondents were asked about the major commodities they shipped to or received from other islands, and the present method of handling such shipments. Then they were asked how they would handle their inter-island shipments if they had a choice of existing facilities or each of the proposed ferry systems: an air ferry, a conventional surface ferry, and a hydrofoil ferry. Questions were also asked about the frequency of making shipments, commodity rates used, sizes of their shipments during the past year (although little information was obtained about the latter), and reasons for wanting to shift from present method of shipping cargo to a ferry.

In very brief summary, respondents indicated a substantial shift in shipment from existing facilities to the proposed ferries. With an air ferry there would be a considerable shift from air freight to an air ferry. Respondents indicated that they would make major shifts from the barge to a conventional surface ferry and to a lesser extent to a hydrofoil ferry. There was also expected to be some increase in inter-island shipments especially with a conventional ferry in operation. Respondents indicated that the major reason for shifting to proposed ferries would be the anticipation of lower rates; other reasons mentioned most frequently were (a) time and speed; (b) better handling; (c) dissatisfaction with existing barge; (d) dissatisfaction with existing air freight; and (e) increased frequency of service.

While the Craig study marked a step forward by surveying households, out-of-state visitors, and business firms, it did not conduct especially sophisticated surveys in design, selection of respondents, structure of questionnaire, and analysis of the problem. Some of the limitations of the surveys were as follows:

a. In all the surveys there were general questions about preferences for existing facilities and an air ferry, a conventional sea ferry, and a hydrofoil ferry. The different types of ferries did not have an adequate description.

25

Moreover, the questions about the hydrofoil had little meaning, since the available evidence was that it was not technically feasible at that time. The preference expressed for the hydrofoil by the respondents was probably based upon the novelty more than anything else.

b. Related to the above point, the choice of existing airlines and each of the three proposed ferries in the survey of households made the results of the survey highly imprecise and little more than an opinion survey. From the standpoint of sampling theory and design, it was improper procedure. It would require three random sub-groups and more sophisticated questions to obtain valid results.

c. In view of the character of the survey, no precise estimates of demand for passenger travel or cargo shipments could be made from it.

d. Moreover, no basis was provided for determining diversion of passengers from existing airlines to a ferry or induced demand by a new system of transportation.

e. Very little confidence can be placed in the results from the survey of out-of-state visitors. The selection of 27 Waikiki hotels by a random method had little meaning. The response by about 14 per cent of questionnaires left at these hotels is hard to evaluate. One question is how representative was this group; it could be highly biased. Moreover, not much reliance could be given to the responses in view of limited descriptions of the proposed ferry services and the types of questions asked. In order to have somewhat meaningful responses, the questions would probably have to be asked by interviewers. Also, the survey was completed during an off-season time of the year for tourism.

f. The survey of business firms and agricultural interests had the limitations of the other surveys previously mentioned; in addition, it was not in any way a random survey. No explanation is given about the method used to select firms. Also, the survey failed to ask some of the most meaningful questions.

26

Parsons, Brinckerhoff, Quade and Douglas report.--Demand and revenue forecasts for ocean and air ferries were made by Professor Kirkpatrick for this report. Professor Kirkpatrick based his demand projections on data derived by the Craig survey and also some of the concepts used in other reports. While he recognized some of the limitations of the Craig report, he felt that since it had surveyed households on their possible use of an ocean ferry described to some extent with specific rates, it provided a rational basis along with other data--especially family income--to estimate passenger demand.

Professor Kirkpatrick emphasized more than other studies that the key to demand for a ferry service was island residents traveling with their cars. He felt that previous studies had not given adequate attention to this. He also emphasized the seasonal character of anticipated travel by families with their cars and felt that the peak demand during the summer months had to be adequately considered in the operation and scheduling of a ferry service.

Professor Kirkpatrick stated that his demand projections were preliminary; but his final report has not yet been completed. He did not state the precise method he used to project passenger and automobile demand for selected years, including 1965 and 1970. In his judgment previous studies had underestimated demand because of deficiency in methods used or failure to consider key aspects of the problem. He said that a ferry service would induce increased travel by island residents with cars, but he did not state how this could be determined. To determine his demand projections he said that he used the Craig survey results as a starting point and also considered family income and other data; moreover, he took into account that a ferry service would more likely lead to considerable family travel with cars. In some ways, he said that it might be more rational to start with an estimate of the number of automobiles and move to an estimate of the number of passengers rather than the other way around. He estimated that it would be reasonable to expect 2.5 passengers per trip with a car and to expect an average annual growth in passenger

travel of 5 per cent. He also considered whether all families would make repeat trips in future years. On the basis of the Craig survey, he estimated that 50 per cent of travel of island residents would take place in the summer months, June to August. Moreover, his estimates based on the Craig survey anticipated that there would be considerable travel--about one-third of the total--from the neighbor islands to Oahu. The demand projections did little to estimate travel by out-of-state visitors on a ferry and cargo demand. They assumed that 10 per cent of out-of-state visitors going to the neighbor islands would use the ocean ferry. They also seem to have accepted the findings of the Craig survey with some adjustments, that 40 per cent of certain types of cargo would be diverted from the barge to the ferry.

It is noteworthy that Professor Kirkpatrick's demand and revenue estimates were substantially higher than those in other studies. His projections of passenger and automobile traffic on a ferry in 1965 were generally three to four times greater than the estimates made in the Law and Wilson-Tudor study for the same year. They were generally two to three times greater than the Law and Wilson-Tudor passenger estimates for 1970.

These demand estimates, in our judgment, have little validity because they were based on the weak foundations of the Craig survey. As we mentioned previously, the Craig survey did not provide a sound basis for making any demand projections because it was deficient in design of the survey, structure of the questionnaires, and in other ways. Professor Kirkpatrick fails to recognize the inherent and fundamental weaknesses of the Craig survey. He also fails to explain adequately how he modified the findings of the Craig survey to obtain his final demand projections.

28

Inter-island ferry system public opinion.--A public opinion poll was conducted on September 9 to 11, 1963 to determine attitudes and preferences of Hawaii residents concerning modes of inter-island transportation and an inter-island ocean ferry. Under the direction of Professor Tuttle, trained University of Hawaii students distributed on a house-to-house basis and collected specially developed questionnaires, which were completed in secret by members of families.

The method used to distribute questionnaires was pin-point sampling. Key polling areas including eight precincts on Oahu, four on Hawaii, three on Maui, and two on Kauai were selected after extensive analysis of the 1956, 1958, and 1959 election returns. Pin-point sampling in these areas had been found highly reliable in predicting previous elections. Following carefully worked-out instructions, students obtained the required number of responses within the polling areas. The total sample was 2,369, with 1,332 from Oahu and 1,037 from the neighbor islands.

The key questions, completed by the respondents in secret, asked about the number of trips taken by the family to the other islands during the past year; whether the trips were on business, pleasure, or both business and pleasure; the preference with respect to travel by air or ocean ferry; and whether the family would like to take their automobile with them to a neighbor island. Questions were also asked whether the State of Hawaii should spend tax money to get an inter-island ocean ferry into operation and spend tax money to build cabins in parks on each island; what are priorities in spending tax money; when are vacations taken; how much was spent on the last vacation; and what are vacation habits.

In brief, the survey showed widespread inter-island travel. A little over a half of the households contacted had made at least one trip to one of the neighbor islands during the last year. Almost four-fifths of the respondents stated that they preferred airplanes for inter-island travel, while less than one-fifth

expressed preference for an ocean ferry. This finding was reinforced by the fact that almost 70 per cent of the respondents said that a low-cost skybus was all the additional transportation required in Hawaii.

Despite the widespread support for air travel, there were some inconsistencies expressed by the respondents. Almost two-thirds of the respondents, especially those living on Oahu, stated that they would like to take their cars with them at reasonable cost on vacations on the neighbor islands. This is obviously something that could be offered by a sea ferry. Furthermore, almost half of the respondents supported the expenditure of tax money to get an ocean ferry in operation. Still, an ocean ferry was quite far down the list in priority in the expenditure of tax money.

Some other useful information was obtained about other aspects relevant to inter-island transportation. Somewhat over half of the respondents were in favor of the state spending tax money to build cabins in state parks on the neighbor islands. Respondents indicated that about 40 per cent of vacation trips were during the three months of June, July, and August. The median amount spent by families on their most recent vacation was about $180; still almost 40 per cent of families reported no expenditures on vacations.

Although the survey compiled an abundance of tables, in many respects it contributed even less than the Craig survey to ascertaining passenger demand for an ocean ferry service. It also contributed little basis for responsible public decision-making on the issue. While pin-point sampling may have some validity in ascertaining opinions of voters with respect to candidates in a forthcoming election, the method as used has little validity in ascertaining public views or future intentions with respect to anything as complicated as demand for an inter-island ocean ferry system. Among the many limitations of this survey, the following are some of the more important ones:

a. It is doubtful that polling areas in key precincts selected from previous elections are relevant with respect to ascertaining views of Hawaiian families on preferences for and possible use of an inter-island ocean ferry system. The results are likely to be less valid than those ascertained in a carefully designed probability sample. Therefore, no interval estimates of passenger demand could be made from the survey.

b. The method of distributing and collecting questionnaires seems open to considerable bias in the results with respect to some of the key questions.

c. The structure of the questionnaire contributed to the vagueness in the results. No precise description was provided respondents on a ferry service including the type of ships, routes, frequency of service, rates, and other key factors. The respondents were simply asked to state broad preferences to very general questions. At best, some general and imprecise opinions could be ascertained from respondents about modes of inter-island transport.

d. The completion of the questionnaires by the respondents themselves in secret also contributed to imprecision in the results and made the survey little more than a very broad opinion survey. The method may also have led to superficial answers without serious consideration of the issues. In contrast, questionnaires administered by highly trained interviewers may lead to more considered answers by respondents to key questions.

e. Related to (d) above, the limitation of the method is also indicated by the inconsistencies of the respondents to some of the key questions.

f. About 30 to 40 per cent of the respondents did not answer some of the questions.

Coverdale and Colpitts report.--This report estimated demand for passenger travel on a surface ferry after considering air travel by island residents and tourists, data available from surveys and previous studies, travel patterns on the

mainland, and passenger travel on other ferries. The report clearly distinguished between passenger travel diverted from the airlines and new travel induced by the availability of a low-cost method of mass transportation for island residents with their cars. It determined that the passenger traffic diverted from the airlines would primarily consist of pleasure and non-business travel by island residents, estimated to comprise about 9 per cent of total airline travel between Oahu, Kauai, Maui, and Hawaii in 1962. It also expected that most passenger autmobiles, except those being shipped by dealers, would be diverted to a ferry.

On the basis of the type of ferry service it proposed, considering frequency of service and length of voyage, and assuming passenger comfort, the report estimated that 20 per cent of pleasure and non-business travel by island residents would be diverted to the surface ferry at optimum fares, that it determined as 70 per cent of existing airline rates. A major consideration in this diversion estimate was the convenience involved for a family on a vacation trip to drive their car loaded with baggage on a ferry, board it, and drive their car off at their destination. The report estimated that only 5 per cent of out-of-state visitors and 5 per cent of Hawaii residents traveling on business would divert from air to ferry travel at optimum ferry fares.

The report also estimated the vacation passenger travel by island residents that would be induced by the operation of a ferry service providing lower cost, convenient travel for people with their cars. In making this estimate, the study found that statistics on Hawaii residents taking vacations on other islands conflicted in various surveys. After making its analysis of available data, it determined that the best estimate was that about 9 per cent of Hawaiian households took vacations on other islands. Examining data from various surveys and studies concerning vacation travel in the United States, average family income and car ownership in Hawaii compared to those on the mainland, and some possible trends, the report

estimated that it was reasonable to expect that with a surface ferry in operation about 15-20 per cent of Hawaii residents would take vacations on other islands in the long run--by around 1972. It expected that this vacation travel to other islands would be induced gradually over time by the operation of the Hawaii State Ferries.

The total passenger demand, therefore, was estimated to consist of that diverted from air travel, especially Hawaii residents on non-business trips, and to a minor extent Hawaii residents on business and out-of-state visitors and also induced travel by Hawaii residents. The study made estimates of passenger traffic at optimum rates--70 per cent of existing airline rates--and also at the lower Hulten Committee rates--about 30 per cent of existing airline rates. It also projected an average rate of increase in passenger traffic of 4 per cent a year in making its demand estimates up to 1972. It compared its estimates of passenger demand for a ferry with traffic on the M. V. Princess of Tasmania between Melbourne and Devonport, Tasmania in Australia. On the basis of its projections about 11 per cent of total Hawaii inter-island travel would be by a sea ferry in 1972, at its optimum rates. This was within the range of travel on some other major routes, providing both sea and air travel. In estimating automobiles carried by a sea ferry, the study used a ratio of 22 cars per 100 persons, similar to that experienced by the Tasmania ferry service.

With respect to cargo, the report emphasized that the ferry was primarily to transport passengers with their cars and was not well suited to handling freight because of short turn-around time and other factors. It did not believe that the ferry could handle the type of freight carried by Young Brothers barges. It expected that most of the freight carried by the ferries would be diverted from Hawaiian Airlines. It estimated that 20 per cent of cargo carried by Hawaiian Airlines would be diverted to a sea ferry at rates comparable to or somewhat below

existing air rates. It expected that most of this would be palletized cargo handled by a fork-lift truck operated by Hawaii State Ferries and also possibly on trucks carried by a ferry.

The Coverdale and Colpitts' method of making demand estimates was essentially a highly conservative one based upon some arbitrary assumptions. However, more than other studies, it emphasized that total passenger demand comprised passenger traffic diverted from the airlines and also induced travel by a ferry service.

The study also considered inter-island vacation travel by Hawaii residents compared to the rate of vacation travel by mainland residents, average family income, car ownership, passenger traffic on other ferries, expected growth of inter-island travel, and other factors. However, there was very little analysis of these factors.

In summary, the demand estimates had some basic limitations:

a. They were not based clearly on the sea ferry service provided by their description, considering the vessels, routes, frequency of service, and other factors. In fact, the demand projections were made independent of the nature of the service.

b. The data used by the report on air travel is not fully consistent with other data available.

c. The report used a number of ratios in their estimates without sufficient empirical evidence or justification--that 70 per cent of airline travel by Hawaiian residents was business travel and 30 per cent was non-business; that about 20 per cent of Hawaiian residents on inter-island non-business trips, about 5 per cent of residents on business trips, and 5 per cent of out-of-state visitors at optimum rates would shift to a ferry; and that the number of automobiles to passengers in a ferry would be the same as for the Tasmania ferry despite the fact that average car ownership is much higher in Hawaii than in Australia. The ratios used kept down the estimate of passenger demand for a ferry service to low levels.

d.   The analysis of demand for cargo was completely inadequate.   The report
was probably incorrect in stating that the type of cargo carried by Young Brothers
barges could not be properly handled by a ferry and that the cargo diverted would
largely be that carried by Hawaiian Airlines.   Actually, the report did not make
any commodity study and hardly analyzed the matter of carrying cargo on a ferry.

In Table I-1, we show the passenger and cargo demand estimates for 1970 in the
three major recent reports: (a) the Law and Wilson-Tudor; (b) Professor Kirkpatrick
for Parsons, Brinckerhoff, Quade and Douglas; and (c) Coverdale and Colpitts.
Table I-2 shows the revenue estimates for 1970 by the same three studies.

3.   Analysis of Cost Estimates

The costs of a ferry system may be considered in terms of the long-term
investments required in ships, terminals, and harbor facilities and the annual
costs.   The annual costs will be related to the capital costs and the type of bond
issue to raise the necessary funds, the interest rates, the terms of the bonds,
the provisions for amortization and other factors.   Annual costs will also depend
upon the characteristics of the ships, type of service provided including routes
and frequency of service, crew requirements, maintenance and repair, the method of
operation and other factors.   Costs may also be related to the passenger and cargo
traffic anticipated.

Thus, cost estimates to the extent that they were undertaken in previous
studies were based upon the description of a ferry system.   However, very few of
the studies made any reliable cost estimates.   The Law and Wilson-Tudor report
made the most comprehensive estimates of capital and annual costs.   The Parsons,
Brinckerhoff, Quade and Douglas report used cost estimates by George C. Sharp, Inc.,
and also data developed by the Law and Wilson-Tudor report.   Coverdale and Colpitts
made use of previous cost estimates in its report.   Careful analysis shows that all

35

TABLE I-1

COMPARISON OF ESTIMATES OF ANNUAL DEMAND FOR A WATER FERRY SERVICE IN 1970

	Law and Wilson-Tudor Preferred Water Ferry Plan		Professor Kirkpatrick for Parsons, Brinckerhoff Quade and Douglas	Coverdale and Colpitts[1]	
	With Transportation Program	With Government Program		Optimum Fares	Hulten Committee Fares
Number of Passenger Trips between:					
Hawaii-Maui	65,600	98,400	164,566	N.A.	N.A.
Maui-Molokai	95,600	143,200	225,235	N.A.	N.A.
Molokai-Oahu	101,600	152,400	229,196	N.A.	N.A.
Oahu-Kauai	49,800	74,800	76,177	N.A.	N.A.
Total Passenger Movement between Two Islands	312,600	468,800	695,174	N.A.	N.A.
Total Passengers One-way Trip	158,600	237,900	333,499	116,000	194,000
Number of Automobiles Shipped One-way between:					
Hawaii-Maui	17,400	26,200	39,272	N.A.	N.A.
Maui-Molokai	25,400	38,200	55,698	N.A.	N.A.
Molokai-Oahu	27,000	40,600	56,799	N.A.	N.A.
Oahu-Kauai	13,200	20,000	16,107	N.A.	N.A.
Total Autos Moved between Two Islands	83,000	125,000	167,876	N.A.	N.A.
Total Autos on One-way Trips	42,000	63,500	75,209	25,520	42,680
Cargo					
Number of Revenue Tons	639,820[2]	827,153[2]	81,062	[3]	[3]

[1] It should be noted that the Coverdale and Colpitts proposed ferries would not stop at Molokai.

[2] Calculated from estimates for 1965 with a 3 per cent annual increase to 1970.

[3] The Coverdale and Colpitts report suggested palletized cargo so that it was not comparable. The report did not give the exact cargo estimate for 1970 but estimated that the cargo would be approximately 20 per cent of the 1962 air freight which amounted to 24,301,000 pounds. No factor was given for the estimated increase in air cargo to 1968 the first year of the ferry operation. After 1968 a 6 per cent per annum increase was estimated for revenue.

N.A.: Not available (only totals available).

Sources: Law and Wilson-Tudor Engineering Company, State of Hawaii Transportation Plan. pp. 114 and 117-118. Parsons, Brinckerhoff, Quade and Douglas, Hawaiian Inter-Island Ferry Study, Final Report, Table 1 and Table IV. Coverdale and Colpitts, Report on the Proposed Hawaii State Ferries, pp. 5, 17, and 20-21.

36

TABLE I-2

COMPARISON OF ESTIMATES OF ANNUAL REVENUES FROM A WATER FERRY SERVICE IN 1970
(Thousands of Dollars)

	Law and Wilson-Tudor Preferred Water Ferry Plan[1]		Professor Kirkpatrick for Parsons, Brinckerhoff Quade and Douglas[3]	Coverdale and Colpitts[4]	
	With Transportation Program	With Government Program[2]		Optimum Fares	Hulten Committee Fares
Passengers	$1,236		$1,963	$1,153[5]	$ 935[5]
Concession	46		966	35	58
Auto	490		536	535	144
Cargo	782		47	190	190
Total	$2,554		$3,512	$1,913	$1,327

[1] After 5 per cent Public Utilities tax.

[2] Not calculated for this year.

[3] After taxes.

[4] Before taxes.

[5] Assume all 5 per cent discount applied to passengers.

Sources: Law and Wilson-Tudor, State of Hawaii Transportation Plan, p. 119. Parsons, Brinckerhoff, Quade and Douglas, Hawaii Inter-Island Ferry Study, Final Report, Table V. Coverdale and Colpitts, Report on the Proposed Hawaii State Ferries, p. 22.

the annual cost estimates are largely based on those developed by the Law and Wilson-Tudor study. We turn now to a brief examination of these cost estimates.

Law and Wilson-Tudor report.--The study first made a comprehensive examination of the costs of ships and construction of terminals and harbor facilities in its Preferred Water Ferry Plan. It estimated that the costs of constructing the ships would be about $6,000,000 each and the port and terminal facilities about $7,000,000. It suggested financing the costs of the ships by a general obligation bond issue of $12,000,000 for 25 years, estimated as the normal life of ships. It proposed a second general obligation bond issue of $7,000,000 for 30 years to finance the terminal and harbor construction, as the estimated life of these facilities was longer. Interest rates were assumed to be 4 per cent on both bond issues.

The study examined the following types of annual costs: (a) debt service charges; (b) costs of operating ships and maintaining port facilities; and (c) administrative expenses. The debt service charges were based on level-fixed payments to amortize the bonds over their life. The annual operating costs consisted primarily of crew wages and subsistence, ship stores, supplies and equipment, fuel oil, maintenance of ships and shoreside facilities, and insurance. Minimum crews of 24 persons were provided to man the ships. Administrative expenses provided for minimum personnel and office expenses to operate the ferry system. The report recommended operation of the ferry system by a private company, including possibly the company now running the inter-island barge, in order to keep down administrative expenses.

In general, the analysis of costs was a mechanical engineering and accounting approach. There was no economic analysis of costs and some factors were not considered.

It was apparently assumed that all costs were fixed regardless of the level of operation. Amortization of principal was considered to be a cost. However, this seems to be a customary practice in these types of financial analyses involving a bond issue. Although amortization is not a cost but rather a provision for payment of debt, it may be considered to be the equivalent of depreciation. However, there was practically no discussion of depreciation. Moreover, the report provided for no increase in costs in the period 1965 to 1980.

The study calculated annual costs for fiscal year 1965, the first year of a possible operation of a surface ferry system and kept annual costs constant until 1980. It did not provide for any rise in labor and other costs. On the other hand it did anticipate growth in ferry revenue. Thus, the deficit was eliminated by 1977 as costs remain constant and revenue increases about 3 per cent a year. This may have been valid procedure, but the report failed to explain its assumptions. For example, the study does not make clear whether costs are calculated in 1960 dollars or 1965 dollars. However, from recent conversations with executives who worked on the study we learn that costs were increased to 1965 and are shown in constant 1965 dollars.

Furthermore, the study assumes that drydocking of the ferry ships would be performed in Oahu. There are no private drydocking facilities for handling the type of ships proposed for the ferry. The only facilities which could handle these ships would be the Navy at Pearl Harbor. But the Navy customarily handles such ships only in the case of emergency. It would require special arrangements with the Navy to drydock the ferry ships. There are other cost items that are not adequately explained. Finally, the cost estimates appear to be minimum cost estimates in constant 1965 dollars.

39

The Law and Wilson-Tudor report also made annual cost estimates for an air ferry system. These cost estimates involved considerably smaller annual costs and smaller deficits than a sea ferry, primarily because an air ferry does not involve heavy investments in terminal and port facilities. As a result, the report recommended the air ferry rather than the sea ferry.

Other reports.--George C. Sharp, Inc., a marine design company made the cost estimates for the Parsons, Brinckerhoff, Quade and Douglas report. In essence, it reviewed the annual cost estimates made in the Law and Wilson-Tudor report. It essentially used the same method and largely the data developed in the Law and Wilson-Tudor study. The major difference in the cost estimates were that they were adjusted to the type of ships and the ferry service that were recommended in the Parsons, Brinckerhoff, Quade and Douglas study. Annual cost estimates were made for the combinations of ships proposed and also for several one-ship trial ferries.

The Coverdale and Colpitts study generally based its cost estimates on those made in the Law and Wilson-Tudor and other reports with some adjustments to reflect differences in the ships and service proposed. It made estimates of capital costs and annual operating expenses, but not total annual costs. The capital cost estimates were kept under $12 million by having one new and one converted used ship and minimal terminal facilities at ports already in use. The report proposed ferry service between Honolulu, Kahului, Hilo, and Nawiliwili.

The costs of the converted Empire State and the annual costs of operating the ship were estimated by the George C. Sharp, Inc., for the Coverdale and Colpitts report. The annual costs of operating the new ship and other costs were based on the Law and Wilson-Tudor report. The Coverdale and Colpitts report assumed a 5 per cent annual increase in labor costs and a 1.5 per cent annual increase in other costs. The average annual increase of 5 per cent for all types of labor costs seems to be excessive. Specifically, it does not seem appropriate to apply the

same cost increase factor for all types of labor, including administrative and operating personnel. Moreover, the study seems to have made an error in escalation of costs. According to information we have received from executives who worked on the Law and Wilson-Tudor report, they provided for increase in costs to fiscal year 1965. Coverdale and Colpitts in their calculations provided for cost increases from 1962 to 1968, the first possible year of operation of a ferry system. Thus, there seems to be a double escalation of costs from 1962 to 1965. A major gap in the report was that it did not consider debt service charges, including interest and amortization of bond debt. However, Eastman Dillon, Union Securities & Co., in a separate letter provided some data on possible revenue bond issue including debt service charges.

Thus, in essence the recent reports that have made annual cost calculations based them on similar engineering and accounting methods. A comparison of the annual cost estimates made in the (a) Law and Wilson-Tudor, (b) Parsons, Brinckerhoff, Quade and Douglas, and (c) Coverdale and Colpitts reports for the first full year of operation of a sea ferry is shown in Table I-3.

4. Summary and Comments

We have already seen that earlier studies leave serious gaps in the treatment of the subject.

In the first place, the description of the proposed ferries varied a great deal, especially with respect to mode of transport, the type and frequency of service, the routes, and the rates charged. Although divergent or even conflicting proposals on such matters may be desirable at the initial stage, they do not permit a unified, systematic, and comprehensive analysis of the multiple aspects of a complex decision problem such as the one involved in an inter-island ferry.

41

TABLE I-3

ESTIMATES ANNUAL COSTS OF A FERRY SYSTEM
IN PREVIOUS REPORTS, FISCAL YEAR, 1965[1]
(Thousands of Dollars)

	Law and Wilson-Tudor	Parsons Brinckerhoff Quade and Douglas[2]	Coverdale and Colpitts[3]
Debt service charge on vessels	768	749	
Debt service charge on shoreside facilities	405	405	
Operation and maintenance of vessels	2,115	2,029	2,450
Maintenance of terminals	50	50	133
Operation of terminals	160	160	
Administration and overhead	165	165	288
Operator's return	--	60	
Total	3,663	3,618	2,871

[1] The Law and Wilson-Tudor report and that by Parsons, Brinckerhoff, Quade and Douglas made projections based on fiscal year 1965 as the first year of operation of a ferry service. The Coverdale and Colpitts report made estimates based on fiscal year 1968 as the first year of operation. We have adjusted these estimates to a 1965 fiscal year basis.

[2] This was based upon one new 23.5 knot ferry ship and one new 16 knot ferry ship, proposed by the study. Other costs estimates were made in the report for other combinations of ships and for one-ship trial systems.

[3] The Coverdale and Colpitts report only estimated annual operating and administrative expenses. It did not make any estimates of annual debt service charges.

42

Second, the efforts made to estimate the demand for a ferry service have serious shortcomings. Estimates on ratios observed elsewhere and applied to trends in population, income and other variables of the Hawaiian economy are largely judgmental. Apart from strictly technical limitations involved in such projections, the major one is the fact that they are not based on objectively verifiable evidence obtained from the island residents. Of course, this limitation is overcome by the survey studies which attempted to assess the response of the public to a ferry service. But again the response is not related as much as possible to a clearly defined set of rates and type of ferry service. Thus, the information collected is not meaningful since for each set of fares and type of ferry service there may correspond a different demand schedule.

Third, by comparison the recent studies, such as the Law and Wilson-Tudor report, contain materials more reliable and valuable information on engineering aspects of operations, description of service and costs than they do on potential demand and economic benefits of a ferry system. This concentration on technical aspects and relative neglect of a systematic analysis of the direct as well as indirect expected benefits seem to be the most serious gap in the treatment of the subject. The proposed ferries are looked upon as privately operated concerns. "Would the proposed ferry pay for itself?" they ask; and the analysis rarely goes beyond an examination of expected costs for constructing and operating a ferry and expected revenues from the ferry service.

Admittedly, an attempt was made early in 1964 to fill this serious gap in the analysis of the subject. The report The Economic Impact of an Inter-Island Ferry System, February, 1964 by Lewis Schipper, Department of Planning and Economic Development, dealt with the indirect economic benefits which the economy of the State of Hawaii might enjoy from the establishment of an inter-island sea ferry. Although this report focuses our attention on some of the neglected aspects of the

subject, its conclusions were based entirely on judgmentally determined conversion ratios. We understand that the report was prepared too late and contained too little to satisfy the state legislature for a terminal decision. A revenue bond issue of $12,000,000 for a sea ferry facility authorized by the state legislature was not floated in the financial market. Funds for the present study were appropriated largely because it was recognized that certain important aspects of the subject required additional scrutiny.

44

STUDIES DEALING WITH INTER-ISLAND TRANSPORTATION IN HAWAII

1. Analysis of Inter-Island Ferry System for the Hawaiian Islands, Joseph B. Ward & Associates, Registered Professional Engineers, March 1, 1956.

2. Supplemental Report--Inter-Island Ferry Service, T. H., June 11, 1956, Joseph B. Ward & Associates. $2,500.

3. Market for Inter-Island Surface Transportation Facilities and Services (for the Harbor Commissioners, by John Child & Co.), 1957. $10,340.

4. Progress Report on Transportation and General Plan, prepared by the State Planning Office and the State Department of Transportation, March 1, 1960.

5. Advance Draft of a Report on Inter-Island Transportation, prepared by Law and Wilson-Tudor Engineering Company for the State Planning Office, January, 1961.

6. State of Hawaii Transportation Plan, prepared for the Department of Planning and Research and the State Department of Transportation, by Law and Wilson-Tudor Engineering Company, March, 1961. $147,000.

7. The Market for a New Inter-Island Ferry System, performed for the Department of Planning and Research, State of Hawaii, by Robert S. Craig Associates, April, 1961. $16,000.

8. Hawaii Inter-Island Ferry Study, final report prepared for the State of Hawaii Department of Transportation by Parsons, Brinckerhoff, Quade and Douglas, April, 1962. Interim Ferry Study, Background and Economic Projections. (Unpublished) Kirkpatrick $2,500.

9. Report on an Inter-Island Ferry Service, for the State Department of Transportation, 1963, by George G. Sharp, Incorporated. $12,000.

10. Inter-Island Ferry System, Public Opinion Poll, conducted September 9, 10, and 11, 1963, by Department of Transportation (Dan Tuttle). Approximately $4,000.

11. Report on the Proposed Hawaii State Ferries, January 27, 1964, Coverdale and Colpitts, Consulting Engineers. $14,650.

12. The Economic Impact of an Inter-Island Ferry System, February, 1964. Lewis Schipper, Department of Planning and Economic Development.

13. Hawaiian Islands Passenger Ferry Ships, by Morris Guralnick, Naval Architect and President, Morris Guralnick Associates, Inc., San Francisco, April 14, 1964.

CHAPTER II

DEFINITION OF THE PROBLEM,
RESEARCH DIRECTIVES, AND SCOPE OF THE STUDY

In addition to the strictly engineering and administrative aspects, an inter-island ferry may be an interesting research subject to social scientists. An economist may be concerned with studying not only costs and revenues but also the expected economic effects of a ferry on the state economy. A sociologist may examine such matters as the interaction between the different interest groups which may be favorably or adversely affected by a decision to establish an inter-island ferry, especially by the method of implementing such a decision. A social psychologist may be interested in the attitudes of the public toward an inter-island ferry, especially the extent to which the public's desire for such a ferry is real or aspirational. Finally, a political scientist may be interested in studying the inter-island ferry as an issue involving different and perhaps conflicting philosophies of government, especially the extent to which a decision has been made on the basis of empirical evidence or as a matter of individual belief on certain principles. Indeed, the subject presents a highly complex situation. For, although the mandate from the legislature confines our investigation to the study of the economic aspects of the subject, all the above-mentioned aspects and perhaps many others may have an important bearing on the decision as to whether to initiate an inter-island ferry service and how to implement this decision.

Thus, the researchers spent considerable time and effort to acquire an overall understanding of the situation, to define the problem with respect to the proposed type of ferry and with respect to research directives, to delineate the scope of the study, and to determine the most efficient methodological approach within the limits imposed by available resources and time. Information on these matters was obtained from the resolution of the state legislature (Senate Concurrent Resolution No. 26, Budget Session of 1964) and from consultation with state officials.

46

1. An Inter-island Sea Ferry System

The reader must realize by now that no systematic investigation of the proposed ferry can be carried out without specifying as clearly as possible its major physical, as well as its operational, characteristics.

The objective of the proposed ferry is to offer a daily comfortable, speedy, and inexpensive mass surface transportation service for people, automobiles, and limited cargo (under specified conditions) between the major islands of the State of Hawaii, namely Kauai, Oahu, Molokai, Maui, and Hawaii--a kind of sea-highway similar to the recently established ferry service in Southern Alaska.

Two new identical ocean-going vessels would be provided for this service. Each vessel would be of 370 feet minimum length and would have a sustained speed of about 18 knots. Each ship would be capable of carrying about 500 passengers and 106 regular size passenger cars or 52 highway trailers. In order to secure maximum comfort for passengers, the two proposed vessels would be equipped with fin stabilizers or flume tanks which would be expected to reduce rolling to only 10 per cent of actual listing. Furthermore, it was considered to be highly desirable for the ships to commute from one island to the other by sailing on the leeward side as much as possible. In addition to securing a ride smoother than if the vessels were allowed to sail on the windward side of the islands, this leeward routing would reduce travel time between the islands to a minimum. At the same time, however, leeward sailing would exclude Hilo and Kahului, the two most populous communities outside Oahu, as possible ports of embarkation. On the other hand, inclusion of the two ports would require windward sailing most of the time for a trip from Honolulu to Hilo. In view of the fact that passenger comfort and travel time are considered to be more important than other factors, it was decided to adopt a compromising solution and include in our analysis Hilo as the only windward port of embarkation.

47

As pointed out earlier, the proposed sea ferry provides for nearly daily service to each of the five major islands of the State of Hawaii. This may be accomplished by allowing each ship to complete a round trip to all the islands within a period from 36 to 48 hours. Since Hilo is included in the proposed routing, daily service to the Big Island would be divided between Hilo and a leeward port. An hourly schedule of the proposed routing is a matter of implementing the sea ferry and, therefore, lies outside the scope of this study.

Additional criteria were considered for the selection of landing sites on the leeward side of each island. These criteria were: (a) impact on the economic development of the island; (b) availability or feasibility of landing facilities; and (c) accessibility to road networks. On the basis of these criteria and after careful study in consultation with various state departments, the following landing sites were considered.

Island	Landing Site
Kauai	Nawiliwili Harbor
Oahu	Honolulu Harbor
Molokai	Kaunakakai
Maui	Maalaea
Hawaii	Kawaihae
	Hilo Harbor

Also, it was realized that the establishment of the proposed sea ferry must be accompanied by the development of recreation and vacation facilities in the islands in carefully selected locations. These facilities would include low-rent cabins which would be available primarily to island residents. It is expected that luxury resort facilities would not be adversely affected by proper and careful planning of the proposed facilities for island residents.

In view of the plans proposed by the state government, it is appropriate to look upon the inter-island sea ferry as a system. This term will be used to

denote the construction and operation of the proposed two vessels, the landing sites, and the recreation and vacation facilities. Also, it may include other elements which, in the course of our research, we may consider to be an integral part of such a system.

2. Directives for Research

In addition to specifying the major physical and operational characteristics of the proposed ferry system, a systematic investigation of it requires a clear understanding of the areas to be covered. This is especially desirable in this study which, as we have already pointed out, presents a highly complex situation. With respect to the areas of investigation, the previously mentioned resolution of the state legislature specifies the following: "...the report on the effect of such a system on the economy of the State of Hawaii shall include, but not be limited to, consideration of the effect of such a ferry system on each of the following factors on a year-by-year basis over a 15- to 25-year period:

a. Personal income;

b. Employment;

c. Hawaii's balance of accounts with the mainland and other areas;

d. The value of land and capital investments;

e. Tourism;

f. State and county tax revenues;

g. The economies of the neighbor islands; and

h. Existing privately-owned commercial, inter-island airlines and barge lines, and such report shall include data on the specific rate structure and type and frequency of operation which will maximize the contribution of the system to the economy of the State of Hawaii;..." Clearly the mandate of the state legislature puts emphasis on a study of the expected indirect economic benefits of the ferry system to the state economy. On the other hand, it leaves to the discretion of the researchers

to define the overall research directives by pointing out that the report should

not be limited to these areas. In the light of our experience from the analysis

and evaluation of the earlier reports and after discussion of such matters with

representatives of the state government, we came to the conclusion that the pro-

posed ferry system raises two fundamental questions:

First, would the ferry system pay for itself and, if not, what is the

expected deficit over time?

Second, if the ferry system requires a state subsidy, what would be the

expected indirect economic and non-economic benefits to the state economy?

Our attempt to answer the above two questions requires an investigation of

the ferry system as a privately operated concern as well as a utility serving

the public. Such an investigation should require coverage of the following broad

areas:

a. A profit and loss analysis of the ferry system which primarily involves

cost and revenue estimates.

b. A study of the economic benefits which the private, as well as the

public sectors of the state economy, are expected to receive from the proposed

state ferry. Most of the areas of investigation falling under this topic have

been specified by the above quoted resolution of the state legislature.

c. An analysis of the social impact which a ferry system may have on the

State of Hawaii.

Such a social study may involve an examination of the expected effect of the pro-

posed ferry system on the social, attitudinal, and political relations of indi-

viduals as well as of racial and interest groups of the islands. Although the

social impact of the proposed ferry system cannot be translated into dollars and

cents, in view of the colorful social history and the unique racial composition

of the islands, these non-economic aspects should not be ignored.

3. Scope of the Study

If this report is destined to be terminal, then our research effort must cover all three above-mentioned broad areas of investigation. But the degree of coverage, quantification, and analytical depth in research is largely a direct function of available resources and time. Furthermore, together with the empirical situation at hand, these variables limit the methods which may be used. Hence, one of our basic problems was to determine how to allocate our effort and time in such a way as to maximize the amount of information which we could possibly collect and analyze for answering the two fundamental questions of our inquiry. For this purpose we established the following guiding rules.

First, our general policy was to build on the knowledge accumulated by earlier studies rather than to duplicate their work. We borrowed from the experience of earlier researchers on the following conditions:

a. When we felt that such information was methodologically sound.

b. Whenever the restraints of time and resources did not permit us to quantify on objectively verifiable information, we used the judgmental quantitive techniques of earlier studies. In such cases, however, we took special pains to justify fully the method and point out its limitations.

c. When the available information was related to the engineering aspects of the ferry system.

Second, with respect to coverage we focused our attention on the first and second broad areas touching only peripherally the non-economic aspects of the proposed ferry system.

Third, with respect to quantification we attempted to present an analysis

which is based on as much objectively verifiable empirical information as the resource and time constraints permitted. Furthermore, the mandate from the state legislature limited our investigation to the study of a sea ferry system involving two ocean-going ships. We assumed that the study of other means of inter-island transportation such as a skybus or a hydrofoil was outside the scope of our investigation since they do not meet the requirements of a mass transportation facility as specified earlier.

a. We have started with the cost estimates for building and operating the ferry system made by earlier studies. However, we made considerable revisions of previous cost estimates on the basis of more recently available information.

b. For the purpose of estimating expected revenue and the indirect economic benefits expected from the ferry system, two surveys were conducted, one of households and one of business organizations and institutions engaged in inter-island trade. The sampling techniques used for these surveys, as well as the limitations of these techniques, are discussed in the appropriate place.

c. We have seen that the mandate from the state legislature specifies that our report should contain "consideration of the effect of such a ferry system on each...factor such as personal income, employment, etc., on a year-to-year basis over 15- to 25-year period." In order to make such projections, we would have to forecast each of the specified time series without the ferry system and then project them with a ferry system. Other things being equal, the statistical error of forecasting time series increases at an accelerated rate with the lengthening of the forecast period. When a factor such as a new transportation system, in this case a ferry system, is introduced, economic projections are particularly hazardous. More important than that, however, is the fact that assignable causes during and after the first year of operations such as an unforseen increase in labor costs, a serious adverse effect of rough seas on

passengers, or an unpredictable growth in traffic, are likely to break empirical continuity. For these technical reasons we project costs and revenues through the first year of ferry operations only; and our economic analysis is carried out without time series projections. For the same reasons such projections beyond the first year of ferry operations have no empirical basis. However, in order to fulfill the contractual obligations assumed by the Economic Research Center, we have appended an economic model. This model is purely judgmental, based on quantitative foundations which cannot be verified empirically. The purpose of this model is to illustrate the analytical process which could have been made if such empirical information were available.

d. If more resources and time were available, our analysis would have been based on a greater body of objectively verifiable quantitative information. Also, we might have been able to construct a model incorporating the key variables of the ferry system for simulating its operation under conditions of uncertainty. However, we doubt if a quantitative analysis more sophisticated than the present one would have altered appreciably our major conclusions.

Fourth, in order to meet important deadlines the analytical depth of this report has been curtailed in some respects. For example, instead of reporting the findings of the two surveys in full detail we present summaries of the most important findings only.

Finally, the engineering aspects of the ferry system lie outside the scope of this study. Also, no systematic investigation was made of the administrative problems related to the implementation of the ferry system, if and when approved. Although implementation does not fall within the scope of this study, to the extent that our findings justify, we shall peripherally touch upon the subject.

In sum, this report may be considered terminal in the sense that it attempts

to evaluate all major aspects of the proposed ferry system. With respect to the degree of analytical depth, however, the report may fall short of the expected results largely because of limitations imposed by available resources and time. Yet, as already mentioned, we doubt that this lack of greater analytical depth has altered our conclusions appreciably. In this sense, however, our report may not be considered terminal.

4. A Few Remarks on Reporting

This introductory part of our report sets up the stage for the analysis of the problem; and at this point it may be pertinent to state a few general guides which may help the reader to clearly understand our position and appreciate our findings.

a. We have tried to be constructive and attempted to make a systematic analysis of the situation, without taking a position for or against the proposed ferry system.

b. In view of the large initial investment required and the uncertainties inherent in the financial success of the proposed ferry system after it is introduced, we have emphasized, more frequently than not, a conservative rather than a liberal position.

c. While this report focuses the reader's attention on the expected direct and indirect economic benefits from the proposed ferry system, it should not be construed to reflect the personal political philosophies of government of the researchers.

d. We live in a rapidly changing technological, economic, and institutional world. Not only are capital investments and technologies subject to obsolescence but so are economic reports. It should be recognized, therefore, that further

our findings.

ferry system.

a liberal position.

researchers.

development of new types of transport, reduction in inter-island and trans-pacific air fares, unforseen or uncontrollable operational costs, and many other factors may outdate parts or all of our report.

e. The nature of the subject is such that our findings and conclusions are largely conditional depending on many ifs and buts. Thus, the chances that this report may be misunderstood, misinterpreted, or misquoted are much higher than otherwise might have been the case. It may be wise and certainly desirable for readers who feel that certain points of this report require clarification to get in touch with the researchers before making any public pronouncements.

f. We scrupulously avoided taking the position of decision makers for or against the proposed ferry system. We have examined the facts and on the basis of our professional judgment we present the pros and cons of the situation. Whether a particular legislator of the State of Hawaii decides for or against the proposed ferry depends on the weights he would like to assign to the findings of this report as well as on other considerations.

The remainder of this report has been written along lines already suggested by the above research directives. Part Two contains Chapters III through V which examine the proposed ferry system on a profit and loss basis. Chapters VI through VIII of Part Three analyze the proposed ferry system as a public utility by considering the expected economic and, to a limited extent, the social benefits of the undertaking.

PART TWO

THE FERRY SYSTEM AS A PRIVATELY OPERATED CONCERN

In discussing the directives for research, we pointed out that the first fundamental question to be raised is whether the ferry system will pay for itself and, if not, what the expected deficit may be over time. This question is discussed in detail in Part Two of our report. Chapter III includes estimates of passenger and cargo traffic of the proposed ferry; Chapter IV deals with initial and operational costs; and Chapter V makes a financial analysis of the ferry system on the basis of expected revenues and anticipated costs.

CHAPTER III

TRAFFIC ESTIMATES FOR THE PROPOSED FERRY SYSTEM

For the purpose of estimating the demand for the proposed ferry as well as for analyzing its expected economic effects on the state economy, two surveys were conducted, one of households and one of business establishments engaged in inter-island trade. The quantitative and the limited qualitative information obtained from these surveys have formed, to a very large extent, the empirical basis of the analysis which appears in this report. In this chapter, however, we shall confine our discussion to the description of survey methods and to traffic estimates for the proposed ferry.

1. The Household Survey

Description.--The sample design involving replicated sampling and the interview schedule for this survey were prepared by James C. Byrnes who came here last summer from Washington, D. C.

The survey involved a probability sample of 1,300 households in the State of Hawaii. On the basis of an interview schedule (questionnaire), trained interviewers solicited information from a responsible member of each household about a number of characteristics of the household, such as (1) age and occupation of the head of the household, (2) total income of the household, (3) the number of persons living in the household, (4) the number of trips made by members of the household to the other islands for strictly business, and (5) the number of trips for pleasure and other reasons during the 12-month period from September, 1963 through August, 1964.

In addition to the above control variables, the interview schedule contained questions which were designed to obtain data about the demand for the ferry system. Respondents were shown pictures of a ship similar to the proposed ferries

and allowed to read a description of the proposed service which emphasized the following major points: (a) daily service between Kauai, Oahu, Molokai, Maui, and Hawaii, (b) a design for smooth sailing in rough waters, (c) a restaurant and other facilities on the ship such as nursery supervision of children, movies, games, etc., and (d) passenger and car fares. In order to test the respondents' reactions to the cost of transportation, two sets of the ferry's description were used, the even description specifying passenger fares which represent 70 per cent of air fares presently in effect and the odd description with fares representing 30 per cent of air fares. Although car fares quoted in the even description represented 70 per cent of barge fares, in the odd description auto fares represented only about 17 per cent of barge fares. These descriptions were used in such a way that when the respondent of one household was exposed to the even description the respondent of the neighbor household was exposed to the odd description. This procedure was followed in order to assess the relationship between price and the potential initial demand for the service which might be offered by the proposed ferry system.

Respondents were asked to check on an 11-point scale with values from zero through ten their answers on whether they would use such a ferry service under different conditions. Scale devices of this type have been used often in opinion surveys to record answers which may have an important element of uncertainty that the respondent recognizes. Experience with the use of scales in situations such as the present one suggests that scale responses expressed as a fraction of ten can be interpreted to represent approximately the probability that a respondent will take the action specified by the question. For example, a scale response of five chosen by each of two respondents for the likelihood that a trip will be made was interpreted to mean that one trip could be expected if the condition in the question were realized.

and allowed to read a description of the proposed service which emphasized the following major points: (a) daily service between [Nome], [Kana], [Molokai], [Maui], and [Herald], (b) a design for smooth sailing in rough waters, (c) a restaurant and other facilities on the ship such as nursery supervision of children, movies, games, etc., and (d) passenger and car fares. In order to test the respondents' reactions to the cost of transportation, two sets of the ferry's description were used, the even description specifying passenger fares which represent 70 per cent of the fares presently in effect and the odd description with fares representing 50 per cent of air fares. Although car fares quoted in the even description represented 70 per cent of barge rates, in the odd description auto fares represented only about 17 per cent of barge rates. These descriptions were used in such a way that when the respondent of one household was exposed to the even description the respondent of the neighbor household was exposed to the odd description. This procedure was followed in order to assess the relationship between price and the potential initial demand for the service which might be offered by the proposed ferry system.

Respondents were asked to check on an [inquiline] safe-availability values represent through ten their answers on whether they would match a ferry service under different conditions. Scale devices of this type have been used often in surveys to record answers which may have an apparent element of uncertainty on the respondent's part. Experience with the use of scaling in situations such as the present one suggests that trade responses expressed as a fraction of ten can be interpreted to represent approximately the probability that a respondent will take the action described by the question. For example, a single response of five chosen by each of two respondents for the likelihood that a trip will be made was interpreted to mean that one trip could be made if the condition in the question were realized.

58

Compared to the usual method of asking respondents to choose answers of "yes," "no," "maybe," or "don't know," the use of the scale device in the manner indicated has many important advantages. The respondent is given the opportunity to express his expectations in quantitative terms with the maximum degree of flexibility. In turn, the aggregate response is computed under conditions of uncertainty, i.e., probabilistically, by using individual checks on the scale as weights. Furthermore, the scale device permits straight-forward estimates of the rate at which specified actions may be expected to occur among different groups in the population. There are no known disadvantages in the use of the scale device except for the limitations imposed by the fact that results represent forecasts, or expected actions, based on the explicit and implicit assumptions and conditions of the questions asked. In this connection, the forecast level at which future events may be expected to occur usually understates subsequent real events. The probable underestimation of the absolute level of response, however, is not likely to distort the relative differences between responses to comparable alternative questions in this study.

Respondents also were asked whether they would patronize new vacation areas to be built on each of the main islands both with and without the availability of the proposed ferry. For soliciting their response they were given a description which specified that these areas would include cabins, spacious enough to accommodate whole families, with bath and cooking facilities for about $10 a night, and accommodations for camping in tents or in trailers, as well as other recreational facilities.

Estimates of passenger traffic of state residents.--The 1,300 households which were included in the sample represent an estimated population of approximately 153,000 households. The sampling procedure covered an estimated population of

approximately 163,000 family units and unrelated individuals. The 153,000

households represented in the survey contained approximately 606,000 persons

including 255,000 registered voters.

One important finding of the survey is the relationship between fares and

passenger and car traffic. In all types of traffic, namely, business trips and

household pleasure trips, the difference in the response between fares at

70 per cent and at 30 per cent of air fares was not statistically significant.

In other words, the difference in response may not be actual but may be attributed

to random factors. Thus, the demand for the ferry, as far as price is concerned,

was found to be inelastic, i.e., a 60 per cent reduction in fares is likely to

increase traffic for passengers and cars by much less than 60 per cent. In view

of these findings the presentation of traffic and revenue estimates in this

report are made at 50 per cent of air fares by taking the mid-point of the response,

obtained at 70 per cent and 30 per cent of air fares.

In order to obtain point estimates of passenger traffic for the State of

Hawaii, the sample responses were blown up by a certain procedure provided in

the sample design. Such point estimates at 50 per cent air fares are shown in

Table III-1. During the first year of operation state residents are expected to

make about 97,000 household round trips on the proposed ferry. Of these trips

15,000 will be for strictly business purposes and 82,000 for pleasure or other

than strictly business reasons. The latter figure consists of 44,000 trips

representing new induced traffic and 38,000 representing traffic diverted from

the airlines. It is estimated that of the 44,000 induced trips as much as 9,000

trips represent a net increase in traffic expected to result from the establishment

of vacation sites. The cost of these vacation sites is not considered part of

the cost of the ferry system since the cost will be met from general state and

federal funds. These point estimates (15,000 and 82,000) are unadjusted, i.e.,

60

TABLE III-1

POINT ESTIMATES OF PASSENGER TRAFFIC OF STATE RESIDENTS
AT 50 PER CENT OF AIR FARES

Item	Unadjusted Response (1)	Adjusted Response[1] (2)
1. Number of household round trips		
a) Strictly business	15,000	15,000
b) Pleasure-other	82,000	90,000[2]
Total	97,000	105,000
2. Number of passenger round trips		
a) Strictly business	15,000	15,000
b) Pleasure-other[3]	164,000	180,000
Total	179,000	195,000
3. Number of passenger round trips		
a) Strictly business	15,000	15,000
b) Pleasure-other	171,000[4]	229,000[5]
Total	186,000	244,000

[1] Figures are rounded to the nearest thousand.

[2] Ten per cent adjustment for probable under-reporting.

[3] Assuming 2 persons per trip.

[4] Assuming 2 persons per trip for 66 per cent of household trips and 2.25 persons per trip for 34 per cent of household trips.

[5] Assuming 2 persons per trip for 46 per cent of household trips and 3 persons per trip for 54 per cent of household trips.

they are based on actual responses in the sample. However, there are reasons to believe that the response for trips other than strictly business understates the actual number of such household round trips which are likely to be made. As we have already pointed out, underestimation may be due to the scale device used in the interview schedule. In addition, the experience of interviewers in the field suggests that some respondents failed to disclose their true intentions about using the ferry system unless they were certain that the venture would be self-supporting financially. Hence, the fear that the proposed ferry would involve a subsidy and probably more taxes may have caused them to check a number on the scale which was smaller than the one they might otherwise have checked.

Of course, it is impossible to calculate with certainty the magnitude of this discrepancy. However, the responses to different questions in the interview schedule offer some evidence which allows us to estimate approximately the minimum number of understated trips. On the basis of the survey, the households in the state are estimated to have made about 92,000 trips by air for reasons other than strictly business during the 12-month period prior to the interview. But these same households expected to make only about 83,000 round trips for the same reasons during the 12-month period subsequent to the interview if vacation sites were not available. Since there is no reason to believe that the number of trips subsequent to the interview were likely to be less than the reported trips made prior to this interview, it is reasonable to conclude that the magnitude of the under-reporting is likely to be at least as large as the above difference of 9,000 trips (92,000 - 83,000) which represents a decline of about 10 per cent. Thus, the point estimate of 82,000 trips is adjusted upward by 10 per cent as shown under column 2 in Table III-1.

Household round trips made by airplane prior to the interview for reasons other than strictly business involved an average of about two persons per trip, while those made for strictly business reasons involved only one person. Assuming

the same number of persons per household trip for the proposed ferry system, the total number of passenger round trips which state residents expected to make on the ferry during the first year of its operation may be estimated at 179,000 for the unadjusted response and at 195,000 for the adjusted response. However, the assumption that each household trip on the ferry for reasons other than business would involve two persons on the average is quite unrealistic. These household trips would be likely to involve more than two persons because of the lower fares and the opportunity to take one's own car on the ferry. An average of four persons per household was estimated on the basis of sample information. The fact that there would be more than two persons per household trip on the ferry is substantiated by the findings of the survey. Although no provisions were made to determine the number of persons per expected household trip on the ferry, sample estimates show that those respondents who intend to use the ferry system and take their car with them represent households with air trips averaging about 2.25 persons per trip. Therefore, the number of persons per household trip with a car is likely to be at least 2.25 persons. Since 34 per cent of the respondents, representing household trips for reasons other than strictly business, stated that they would like to take their cars on a ferry trip, this portion of the household trips was multiplied by a factor of 2.25. The remaining portion was multiplied by a factor of two. Thus, the total number of passenger round trips for state residents was estimated at about 186,000 for the first year of ferry operations.

The above estimate is based on the sample response without any adjustments. Admittedly this is an estimate which, for lack of a better term, we shall call a conservative estimate. However, for reasons explained earlier, the number of household trips with a car is likely to be under-reported. This contention is reinforced by the fact that the field workers who interviewed the respondents feel that at least 50 per cent of household trips might involve a car. Furthermore,

on the basis of sample results, respondents who intend to use the ferry and take their own car on a business trip represent 54 per cent of such trips. In addition, the factor of 2.25 persons per household trip seems quite conservative. Using an arbitrary factor of three persons per trip, which is still a conservative factor since there are about four persons per household, for 54 per cent of household trips and a factor of two persons per trip for 46 per cent of household trips, the total number of passenger round trips by state residents may be estimated at 244,000 during the first year of ferry operations. For convenience and for comparison to the conservative estimate we shall call the 244,000 passenger trips a liberal traffic estimate.

It should be noted that the above two passenger traffic figures are point estimates. They do not take into consideration the fact that these figures may underestimate or overestimate the actual traffic intended because of random factors. The sampling technique used in this survey, however, permits us to make interval estimates of this traffic with known degrees of confidence. Such interval estimates for the conservative and the liberal estimates at a 90 per cent degree of confidence are shown in Table III-2. Their meaning is quite important. For example, in the conservative estimate based on the unadjusted response, there is a 90 per cent chance that actual passenger traffic intended by state residents may be no less than 153,000 trips and no more than 219,000 trips during the first year of ferry operations. Although there is a 50 per cent chance that such traffic will be about the point estimate of 186,000 passenger round trips, there is only a 5 per cent chance that traffic will be less than 153,000 trips. The liberal intervals may be interpreted in a similar fashion.

Estimates of automobile traffic for state residents.--The results of the household survey on automobile traffic for the ferry are shown in Table III-3. The conservative estimate of 35,980 cars is based on the unadjusted response

obtained from the survey. Since respondents representing 54 per cent of business trips and 34 per cent of household trips for reasons other than strictly business stated their intention of taking their car on the ferry, the above conservative estimate was obtained by multiplying the 15,000 business trips by a factor of 0.54 and the remaining 82,000 by a factor of 0.34. But we have already explained that there is under-reporting of car trips for pleasure. In fact, the available evidence for under-reporting is much stronger in the case of cars than in the case of household trips. We derived the liberal estimate of 52,380 by multiplying the unadjusted 82,000 household pleasure trips by a factor of 0.54 and adding 8,100 cars for business trips.

TABLE III-2

INTERVAL ESTIMATES OF PASSENGER TRAFFIC OF STATE RESIDENTS
AT 50 PER CENT OF AIR FARES AND 90 PER CENT DEGREE OF CONFIDENCE[1]/

Item	Confidence Limits		
	Lower (1)	Point (2)	Upper (3)
1. Unadjusted response Conservative estimate	153,000	186,000	219,000
2. Adjusted response Liberal estimate	200,000	244,000	288,000

[1]/Figures rounded to the nearest thousand.

Interval estimates of the above point estimates for automobile traffic of state residents is shown in Table III-4. They may be interpreted in the manner explained earlier. For example, under the conservative estimate there is a 90 per cent chance that automobile traffic of state residents will be no less than 29,504 cars and no more than 42,456 cars for the first year of ferry operations. Actually, traffic is most likely to be close to the mid-point of this interval which represents a point estimate of 35,980 cars. On the other hand, there is a 5 per cent chance that such automobile traffic will be less than 29,504 cars or more than 42,456 cars. The confidence limits of the liberal estimates may be interpreted in a similar fashion.

65

TABLE III-3

POINT ESTIMATES OF AUTOMOBILE TRAFFIC OF STATE RESIDENTS

Item	Number of Cars
1. Unadjusted response[1]	
a) Strictly business	8,100
b) Pleasure-other	27,880
Total	35,980
2. Adjusted response[2]	
a) Strictly business	8,100
b) Pleasure-other	44,280
Total	52,380

[1] At 54 per cent of business trips and 34 per cent of household pleasure trips.

[2] At 54 per cent of household, business and pleasure trips.

TABLE III-4

INTERVAL ESTIMATES OF AUTOMOBILE TRAFFIC BY STATE RESIDENTS AND 90 PER CENT DEGREE OF CONFIDENCE

Item	Confidence Limits		
	Lower (1)	Point (2)	Upper (3)
1. Unadjusted response Conservative estimate	29,504	35,980	42,456
2. Adjusted response Liberal estimate	42,952	52,380	61,808

66

Although one description (even) quoted a car fare representing 70 per cent of barge fares and the other (odd) quoted only 17 per cent of barge fares, the difference between responses to the two descriptions with respect to whether the respondent intended to take his own car was not statistically significant.

A few general remarks.--Other important survey findings will be presented later with the analysis of the expected economic effects of the proposed ferry on the state economy. At this point, it is pertinent to make a few remarks on the conditions which must be taken into consideration for interpreting the above survey results.

a. The propensity of the state residents to patronize the proposed ferry system is an expression of intentions. Whether and to what extent their intentions will materialize depends on the assumption that the conditions, such as economic and aspirational, at the time of the interview remain unchanged at the time the ferry system is put into operation.

b. The estimates of intention to travel on the ferry shown in Tables III-1 and III-2 represent annual aggregate potential traffic which may be generated by state residents. They do not take into consideration seasonal variations and their effect on intentions to travel.

c. Furthermore, this propensity to travel on the proposed ferry depends on the assumption that no new transport facilities for passengers, such as a skybus or a hydrofoil, become available for inter-island transportation before the introduction of the proposed ferry.

d. Although the survey results show that the state residents at large are not too price conscious, their estimated propensity to travel on the ferry is based on the assumption that no substantial reduction in air fares will occur before the ferry system is introduced.

e.   According to the field reports from the interviewers, a large majority of the respondents seem to be well aware of the rough waters between the islands. Their doubts were usually accompanied by the remark that they were "willing to give it (the ferry) a try." Thus, the propensity of state residents to patronize the proposed ferry depends <u>to a very large extent on the experience they have during their first trip on the ferry. The incidence of seasickness or the lack of it is the most important unknown single factor which may largely determine whether passenger traffic for the ferry will be sustained and grow.</u>

f.   The intention to travel on the ferry may have been conditioned to a considerable extent by whether or not the respondents considered that the proposed ferry system would be a deficit operation requiring a subsidy and eventually higher taxes.

g.   The above passenger and traffic estimates of state residents are based on the respondents' propensity to patronize the proposed ferry system at the time of the interview if such a system were operating. In fact, the proposed ferry system is not likely to start operating before the end of 1968. Thus, the survey findings must be projected for the year 1969. We shall tackle this problem after we deal with the survey of business establishments.

2.   The Cargo Survey

<u>Introduction.</u>--The resolution of the state legislature specified that in addition to providing a mass transportation facility for passengers and cars, the proposed ferry was supposed to provide a facility for carrying "...freight loads, including fresh produce and similar agricultural products, on as interchangeable a basis as possible..." But the resolution did not and could not specify the conditions, especially those related to loading and unloading cargo and to handling cargo. As we pointed out earlier, traffic estimates for a ferry are bound to lack meaning unless the type of service the ferry would offer to its user is specified as clearly as possible.

68

A great deal of effort was spent in preparing a description of the ferry service for handling cargo. Initially, the proposal was advanced that the two ships of the ferry system would carry cargo on trucks, with roll-on, roll-off handling. While this method of handling cargo has been successful in many ferry systems on the mainland, it has certain disadvantages for the proposed ferry, which will be discussed later. Because of these disadvantages, we considered a modified version of the typical truck or trailer, roll-on, roll-off method of handling cargo.

Under this method cargo in containers, pallets, or bins may be placed on flat cars at points of embarkation in advance of ferry departure time. These flat cars may be equipped with dollies, or the ferry may be inlaid with rails. At loading time, a set or train of flat cars may be pushed aboard or pulled off the ferry at will. This "piggyback" method of handling has certain advantages over the roll-on, roll-off method and a number of disadvantages of its own, which will be discussed later.

In designing the cargo survey we decided to solicit information for both methods of cargo handling.

Survey design and field work.--The cargo survey involves a disproportionate stratified random sample of 100 business establishments engaged in inter-island trade. Although this sample represents only about 15 per cent of credit shippers of Young Brothers, Ltd., it represents about 40 per cent of the tonnage of all Young Brothers' credit shippers and 33 per cent of the total tonnage carried by this company in 1964.

The interview schedule of the survey included certain control variables, such as the type of business carried by each firm, whether or not the firm was engaged in out-of-state trade during 1964, the general types of shipments which each firm had traded with the other islands, etc. But the main objective of the interviews

schedule was to solicit information about whether and to what extent a shipper would use the proposed ferry if either of the two methods of cargo handling described above were employed. Also, the responding executives of each sampled firm were asked about the potential effect which the use of the ferry might have on his inventory and volume of shipments. The same 11-point scale device described earlier was used to solicit responses to these substantive questions.

The description for cargo service specified the ports of embarkation and provided for two routes: one which included the leeward ports only and another which included Hilo and Kahului. The "piggyback" method of cargo handling was described in detail. After the responses were recorded for this method, the respondent's reaction was assessed for the roll-on, roll-off method of cargo handling. Thus, information about cargo traffic for the ferry was obtained for both methods of cargo handling. Furthermore, the description specified that freight rates would be competitive with the existing inter-island cargo rates.

All interviews in the outer islands and the most important interviews on Oahu were conducted by the principal investigators. This extensive and time-consuming field work gave us the opportunity to collect first-hand information for estimating potential cargo traffic. Furthermore, the penetrating analytical comments made by business executives, whose firms are engaged in widely diverse business activities, have been very helpful to the principal investigators for studying the probable economic effects of the ferry on the state economy.

Cargo traffic estimates and related findings.--Point and interval estimates of cargo traffic for the proposed ferry are shown in Table III-5. There is a 50 per cent chance that cargo traffic may be about 36,128 short tons with the roll-on, roll-off method and about 109,082 short tons with the "piggyback" method of cargo handling. There is 90 per cent chance that cargo traffic may be no less than and no more than the tonnage indicated in the lower and upper confidence limits,

respectively, for each method of cargo handling. But there is only a 5 per cent chance that cargo traffic may be less than 29,625 short tons under the roll-on, roll-off and 89,262 short tons under the "piggyback" method.

TABLE III-5

POINT AND INTERVAL ESTIMATES OF CARGO TRAFFIC IN SHORT TONS
AT 90 PER CENT DEGREE OF CONFIDENCE

Method of Cargo Handling	Lower Confidence Limit (1)	Point Estimate (2)	Upper Confidence Limit (3)
1. Roll-on, roll-off	29,625	36,128	42,631
2. "Piggyback"	89,262	109,082	128,902

The difference in tonnage traffic between the two methods of cargo handling is statistically significant. This means that such a difference cannot be attributed solely to random factors, and the question may be raised, what are the assignable causes for such a difference?

a. The above difference in cargo traffic must be largely attributed to the different costs which a business firm must pay for each method of cargo handling. Although the description of ferry service specified that freight rates would be competitive to the existing surface cargo rates, a majority of the respondents pointed out that the roll-on, roll-off method would require additional expense for trucks and trailers. Furthermore, the required rolling stock and personnel are likely to be tied up for more than 24 hours per trip. Thus, many businessmen expressed the opinion that, unless somebody else bears this additional cost, the roll-on, roll-off operation would not be economically feasible. The cargo traffic under the roll-on, roll-off method represents cases where the respondent felt that the additional cost would be less than the economies he expects to

respectively, under each method of cargo handling. But there is only a 5 per cent

chance that RORO traffic may be less than 19,435 short tons under the roll-on-

roll-off and 82,162 short tons under the "piggyback" method.

TABLE III

TOTAL AND INTERVAL ESTIMATES OF CARGO TRAFFIC IN SHORT TONS
AT 90 PER CENT LIMITS OF CONFIDENCE

Method of Cargo Handling	Lower Confidence Limit (1)	Total Estimate (2)	Upper Confidence Limit (3)
1. Roll-on, roll-off	19,435	38,136	67,431
2. "Piggyback"	82,162	109,082	135,902

The difference in tonnage traffic between the two methods of cargo handling

is statistically significant. This means that such a difference cannot be

attributed solely to random factors, and the question may be raised, what are the

reasonable reasons for such a difference?

1. The above difference in cargo traffic may be largely attributed to the

different costs which is chargeable for each method of cargo handling,

although the description of ferry service rendered and the freight rates would be

comparable to the existing surface cargo rates, a majority of the respondents

pointed out that the roll-on, roll-off method would require additional expense

for truck and trailers. Furthermore, the required rolling stock and personnel

are likely to be tied up for more than 24 hours per trip. Thus, many businessmen

interested shippers who handles somewhat piad bears this additional cost, the

roll-on, roll-off service would not be economically feasible. The cargo

traffic under the roll-on, roll-off method represents cases where the respondent

felt that the additional costs would be less than the economies he expects to

realize because of elimination of excessive handling of merchandise, less frequent use or elimination of air shipments, and more reliable and frequent service. On the other hand, the "piggyback" method seems to be more compatible with the present practices of shipping locally grown commodities. Thus, from the standpoint of the responding businessman the "piggyback" method of cargo handling is more economically feasible. Under the "piggyback" method businessmen understood that the ferry system would supply the required flat cars, tractors, and loading facilities with the shipper furnishing their own containers, pallets, or bins.

b. Cargo traffic probably would be greater than the above estimates if Hilo in Hawaii and Kahului in Maui were included among the ports of embarkation. However, it is likely that the additional cargo traffic would be larger under the "piggyback" than under the roll-on, roll-off method, thus widening the above estimated difference in cargo traffic between the two methods.

c. A majority of the respondents pointed out or implied that the government "should not compete with private enterprise." Such a statement seems to be based on the assumption that there can be no alternative to state government management of the proposed ferry system. Aside from the administrative arrangement several respondents felt that such competition is likely to be greater under the "piggyback" than under the roll-on, roll-off method of handling cargo.

A number of general points made by the respondents of the survey which are intimately related to cargo traffic follow.

a. One remark which we have heard repeated frequently is that "passengers and cargo do not mix." A ferry attempting to serve both types of traffic would satisfy neither the passengers nor the shippers.

b. Farmers, managers of farm cooperatives, produce men, and other shippers had mixed reactions with respect to the advantages of a ferry system for carrying their products to the market. Some of these respondents seem especially interested

in an improvement of the existing barge service; others preferred a new and
competitive transportation service. There was also some feeling that a new
containerized operation by Matson Lines would provide all the additional inter-
island cargo service required. A position which was taken by a number of managers
of farm cooperatives and produce men was that other problems relating to production,
processing, and marketing of farm products had a higher priority than the proposed
ferry.

c. In the minds of many of the respondents, there seemed to be a conflict
between the proposed ferry system as a new facility for inter-island movement
of passengers and cargo and the governmental decision to implement the system
which might be contrary to their philosophy of government. Several respondents
said they and their families would use the ferry as passengers. Many of them
thought that the proposed ferry system might help to stimulate the economies of
the neighboring islands. The ferry was generally considered basically good on
the following conditions: a) that it does not seriously disrupt or harm the
existing inter-island transportation carriers; b) that it is not a deficit
operation from the start, requiring a government subsidy which in their opinion
inevitably leads to an increase in the high taxes already existing. Many of the
respondents would be in favor of the proposed ferry with a deficit operation, if
it can be clearly shown that the expected indirect benefits from this venture
outweigh the required subsidy. Quite a few respondents, however, were opposed
to the proposed ferry as a matter of principle and because they felt that it would
be a deficit operation requiring chronic subsidies.

As in the case of passenger traffic, cargo traffic must be projected for
the year 1969. Of course, it is assumed that in the interim no important changes
would take place in the existing barge service and no new service would be
introduced, such as the contemplated new cargo containerized service by Matson Lines.

73

3. Overall Traffic Estimates for 1969

In estimating the overall traffic of the proposed ferry system for 1969, the first year that such a system could be expected to be in operation, we have used the conservative interval estimates of the household and cargo surveys. The reader can very easily make projections on the basis of liberal interval estimates of the two surveys by applying the method used here. In addition, for overall traffic estimates we make judgmental projections of the tourist passenger and automobile traffic for 1969.

Passenger traffic.--If the ferry system had been put into operation immediately after the household survey, it is estimated that the passenger traffic of state residents would be between 153,000 and 219,000 passengers for the year 1965 at 90 per cent degree of confidence (Table III-2). The projections of the above limits are 179,010 and 256,230 passengers, respectively, for 1969 as shown in Table III-6. These projections are based on the conservative compound growth factor of 4 per cent previously used by Coverdale and Colpitts.

The technique of making forecasts from survey data requires the use of a constant measurement method in a series of surveys, say at yearly intervals, and drawing inferences regarding changes from one point in time to another. This technique has worked very well over the past five years to forecast the demand for new automobiles, using the quarterly survey data on intentions to purchase. Thus far, however, researchers are unable to forecast with a satisfactory degree of accuracy from a single survey. It is important, therefore, to note that the above projections of passenger traffic are based on forecasts from a single household and a single cargo survey which reduce the degree of reliability that such projections might have had otherwise.

74

TABLE III-6

OVERALL TRAFFIC ESTIMATES FOR THE PROPOSED FERRY SYSTEM
FIRST YEAR OF OPERATIONS

Kind of Traffic by Source	Interval Limits		
	Lower (1)	Mid-point (2)	Upper (3)
1. _Passenger_			
a) State residents[1]	179,010	217,620	256,230
b) Tourists[2]	56,600	62,180	67,760
Total	235,610	279,800	323,990
2. _Automobiles_			
a) State residents [1]	34,519	42,096	49,674
b) Tourists[3]	2,830	3,109	3,388
c) Commercial[4]	12,443	15,174	17,905
Total	49,792	60,379	70,967

[1] Based on the conservative estimate of the household survey Tables III-2 and III-4 multiplied by a factor 1.17 representing a 4 per cent cumulative growth factor.

[2] The lower limit is based on 821,000 and the upper on 982,000 visitors multiplied by a factor of 6.9 per cent.

[3] Represents a ratio of 20 tourists for one car.

[4] Each commercial vehicle unit represents three short tons of the projected cargo under the roll-on, roll-off method. The tonnages were obtained by projecting the figures in Table III-5 to 1969 at a 6 per cent compound growth factor.

TABLE III-6

OVERALL TRAFFIC ESTIMATES FOR THE PROPOSED FERRY SYSTEM
FIRST YEAR OF OPERATIONS

Kind of Trip by Source	Interval Limits			per
	Lower (1)	Mid-point (2)	Upper (3)	
1. Passengers				
a) State residents [1]	179,010	217,620	256,230	
b) Tourists [2]	56,600	62,160	67,790	
Total	275,610	279,800	323,990	
2. Automobiles				
a) State residents [3]	24,519	42,098	69,0__	6v
b) Tourists [3]	2,630	3,409	3,388	188
c) Commercial [4]	12,943	15,176	17,907	907
Total	45,792	60,3__	70,5__	

1/ Based on the conservative estimate of the probable surveys Tables III-1-2
and III-6 multiplied by a factor 1.1 representing a 6 per cent cumulative
growth factor.

2/ The lower limit is based on 841,000 and the upper on 922,000 visitors
multiplied by a factor of 6.9 per cent.

3/ Represents a ratio of 20 tourists for one car.

4/ Each commercial vehicle unit represents three short tons of the
projected cargo under the 1971 on railroad method. The tonnages were obtained
by projecting the figures in table III-5 to 1969 FC and per cent compound
growth factor.

75

Limitations of time and resources did not permit us to conduct a systematic survey of tourists in order to estimate tourist traffic for the proposed ferry system based on empirically verifiable information. Therefore, our projections shown in Table III-6 are largely judgmental.

During 1964, according to the latest count, the number of visitors who stayed in Hawaii overnight is approximately 510,000. On the basis of a 10 per cent compound growth factor, the number of such visitors during 1969 is expected to be about 821,000. The 10 per cent factor is conservative in view of the fact that since 1959 the number of visitors has increased by a factor of 13 per cent. Of course, this projection assumes that important conditions such as the recent rates of economic growth and prosperity and the $100 air fare from California, which have largely contributed to the increase in the number of visitors, will continue their favorable impact. Also, this projection does not take into consideration that further reduction of air fares within the United States and also from countries of the Far East, especially Japan, may create additional waves of visitors to Hawaii.

The above projection of tourist traffic for the proposed ferry is based on a 10 per cent compound growth factor of visitors. Assuming a 14 per cent growth factor which is more in line with the increases of visitors since 1962, the expected number of visitors for 1969 may be estimated at 982,000.

In the past, more than 40 per cent of the visitors in Hawaii went to one or more neighboring islands. From the household survey we have found that initially 23 per cent (low-point estimate at 90 per cent confidence) of air passenger trips by state residents may be diverted to the proposed ferry system. This diversion ratio is too high for the tourist air traffic. In the first place, the number of nights away from home for household trips of state residents was on the average 7.7 nights per trip according to the household survey. On the other hand, according to the available statistics of the Hawaii Visitors Bureau the average stay on the

neighboring islands for tourist was only 2.6 nights per tourist. Furthermore, on the basis of the household survey under both the conservative and the liberal estimates, half of the non-business total traffic for the ferry would be new or induced and half diverted. Also, our two 1969 projections of 821,000 and 982,000 tourists represent an increase of 61 per cent and 92.5 per cent over the recorded number of 510,000 visitors for 1964, respectively. Thus, we consider that half of the 23 per cent of projected visitors will represent diverted air trips and half new or induced trips to the neighbor islands. Also, by 1969 direct jet flights from California to Hilo may reduce considerably the expected tourist rides on the ferry. On the basis of available information, about 35 per cent of all the visits to the neighbor islands were made to the Big Island. Assuming that as much as 25 per cent of future visits will be made by direct flights to Hilo, then about 6.9 per cent (0.40 x 0.23 x 0.75) of the expected 821,000 or 982,000 visitors may patronize the proposed ferry, or between 56,600 to 67,760 as shown in Table III-6. Although each tourist may ride the ferry to visit more than one neighbor island, we may further assume that on the average each visitor represents a single round trip to one island.

It is important to note that the two projections for tourist passenger traffic do not represent an interval estimate since they are not based on a probability sample. The lower figure is a conservative and the upper a more liberal projection, but both are largely judgmental. On the other hand, the reader may note that the average of our projections, 62,180 tourist passenger trips, is in line with the average of the projections which may be obtained by applying the diversion ratios used by Coverdale and Colpitts.

Automobile traffic.--Assuming the same compound growth factor of 4 per cent used for passenger traffic, the conservative estimate of automobile traffic by state residents may be between 34,519 and 49,674 , as shown in Table III-6. The

neighboring islands for courier duty might particular. Furthermore,

on the basis of the household survey under both the conservative and the liberal

estimates, half of the non-business local traffic for the ferry would be new or

induced and half diverted. Also, our two 1969 predictions of 821,000 and 982,000

tourists represent an increase of 64 per cent and 92 per cent over the recorded

number of 510,000 visitors for 1964, respectively. Thus, we conclude that half

of the 23 per cent of proposed visitors will represent diverted air trips and

half new or induced trips to the neighbor islands. Also, by 1969 direct jet

flights from California to Hilo may reduce considerably the expected tourist rides

on the ferry. On the basis of available information, about 23 per cent of all

the visits to the neighbor islands were made to the Big Island. Assuming that

as much as 25 per cent of future visits will be made by direct flights to Hilo,

then about 6.9 per cent (0.40 x 0.23 x 0.75 of the expected 821,000 or 982,000

visitors may patronize the proposed ferry, or between 56,600 to 67,780 as shown

in Table III-6. Although each courier may ride the ferry to visit more than one

neighbor island, we may further assume that on the average each visitor represents

a single round trip to the island.

It is important to note that the two projections for tourist passenger

traffic do not represent an interval estimate since they are not based on a

probability sample. The lower figure is a conservative and the upper a more

liberal projection, but both are largely judgmental. On the other hand, the reader

may note that the average of our projections, 902,000 tourist passenger trips, is

in line with the average of our projections which may be obtained by applying

the diversion ratio-weighted generated demand supplies.

Automobile traffic. Assuming, on the same comparable basis, for a net cent

used for passenger traffic, the comparative estimate of automobile traffic by

shore residents may be obtained by the same methods reported in Table III-6. The

projections for tourist automobile traffic in the same table represents one automobile for 20 tourist passenger trips. We offer no other explanation for this ratio but our judgment.

The interval estimate of traffic for commercial vehicles shown in Table III-6 was obtained as follows: The estimated cargo for the ferry under the roll-on, roll-off method of cargo handling shown in Table III-5 (29,625 for the lower, 36,128 for the mid-point, and 42,631 for the upper limit of estimate) was projected to 1969 by applying a 6 per cent compound growth factor which Coverdale and Colpitts used earlier in their study. Then the projected figures, 37,328, 45,521, and 53,715, representing the lower, mid-point, and upper estimates, respectively, were converted to commercial vehicle units. Each commercial vehicle unit with length approximately equal to the length of a regular size passenger car was assumed to have a capacity of 1.5 short tons, or 3 short tons for a round trip. The 1.5 short tons is the maximum tonnage which a commercial vehicle of that size can carry. This conversion ratio is used for no other reason but for facilitating estimates of expected revenues which will be discussed in Chapter V. Later, we shall explain why our projections of commercial vehicular traffic are based on the roll-on, roll-off method. The reader, of course, can use the above method to make projections of such traffic for cargo under the "piggyback" method.

Interpretation of projected estimates.--We may recall that projections of passenger traffic for state residents for 1969 were obtained by applying a 4 per cent compound factor to the household estimates. Also, projections of automobile traffic for 1969 were obtained by applying a 4 per cent compound factor to the passenger car traffic of the household estimates and a 6 per cent compound factor to the vehicular traffic estimates of the cargo survey. These projected estimates raise the technical question as to whether to assign the 90 per cent confidence of estimates obtained from the surveys, which involve objective probabilities, to the projected estimates.

78

If the compound factors of 4 per cent and 6 per cent used for these projections are considered as constants, then the 90 per cent confidence may be assigned to the projected estimates for 1969. Under this interpretation of the compound factors, we may assign the objective probabilities which we used earlier for the 1965 estimates. Thus, we may state that there is a probability of only about 5 per cent that passenger traffic of state residents may be less than 179,010 or more than 256,230 with a 50 per cent chance that it may be 217,620. Similar statements may be made for automobile traffic of state residents and for commercial automobile traffic. By contrast, such probabilistic statements based on objective probabilities cannot be made for tourist traffic since our estimates of such traffic are not based on a probability sample.

However, if the compound factors of 4 per cent and 6 per cent used for these projections are considered as random variables, then an additional random error is introduced by these factors. In such a case and according to the objective theory of probability, it is not legitimate to assign objective probabilities to projected estimates. Nevertheless, it is quite legitimate to assign to these projected estimates subjective probabilities. Such probabilities may express the "intensity of belief" that the researchers of this report would like to assign to the occurrence of these projected estimates.

The overall traffic estimates shown in Table III-6 are conservative. This is consistent with our stated condition in Chapter II to emphasize the conservative viewpoint. For the same reason, in discussing the expected profit and loss statement of the proposed ferry system in Chapter V, we shall assign subjective probabilities to the 1969 projected traffic estimates. The reason for this conservative choice, as well as traffic prospects after 1969, is discussed in Chapter V.

79

4. Examination of Factors Which May Affect Traffic

Travel by island residents on a sea ferry should be related to factors such as the following: personal income, disposable personal income, family income, income distribution, transportation and other costs in traveling to other islands, vacation habits and preferences, special attractions offered by the neighbor islands, and alternative types of travel available and their costs. For example, our survey of households shows a high positive correlation between family income and propensity to travel to other islands. We shall, therefore, examine income and other factors below.

Personal income.--As we can see in Table III-7 in the Appendix to this chapter, personal income per capita in Hawaii was $2,493 in 1963--a little higher than the national average. Table III-8 shows that the state ranked 16th among states in the country. Personal income per capita in Hawaii has been increasing more rapidly than in the rest of the country. From 1955 to 1963 it increased at an average rate of a little over 4 per cent per year in Hawaii compared to about 3 per cent in the United States. As Table III-8 in the Appendix of this chapter shows, median family income in Hawaii in 1963 was estimated at $7,680 in 1963, about 8 per cent higher than for the United States as a whole; the state ranked 8th among states in the United States. Median family income is higher in Hawaii because the state has on average more family members working, especially wives in the household. While the median family income is higher in monetary terms, in real terms there probably is not much difference, when it is considered that the cost of living is somewhat higher in the state than the average on the mainland.

For purpose of passenger demand for a ferry service, personal income of Oahu families is of special importance, for they would presumably do most of the traveling. The Bureau of Labor Statistics Survey of Consumer Expenditures and

80

Income of families in Honolulu in 1961 showed that money income per household

after taxes was $7,950 compared to an average of $5,957 for major cities in the

United States.[1] The money income after taxes was higher than the average for

cities in the Northeast, the West, the North Central, and the South. As we can

see in Table III-9 in the Appendix of this chapter, the per cent of savings in

the Honolulu area per household was almost twice the rate in the United States as

a whole and was higher than in any other major area in the country.[2]

From the Bureau of Labor Statistics Surveys, we have made an estimate of

discretionary money income per household for Honolulu and major areas in the

United States. Our definition of discretionary income is total money income

after taxes less the following necessary consumption expenditures and obligations:

food prepared at home, housing, fuel, light, refrigeration, water, household

operations, clothing, medical and personal care, and personal insurance.[3] As

Table III-9 in the Appendix to this chapter shows, from the Bureau of Labor

Statistics Survey data, the discretionary income per household in the Honolulu

area is much higher than the average in large cities in the United States and

in major regions of the country.

Our survey of households showed a high positive relationship between

household income level and the number of trips and the extent of inter-island

[1]Bureau of Labor Statistics, Consumer Expenditures and Income Report,
No. 237-78; in Oshima, Harry T. and Ono, Mitsuo, Hawaii's Income and Expenditures,
1958, 1959, and 1960, Volume II, Economic Research Center, V-23. The B.L.S.
survey is confined to larger cities which contain the poorer families. It does
not include the higher income families in suburbs on the Mainland, but may include
them in Honolulu. Moreover, the B.L.S. income concepts differ from the Department
of Commerce income accounts.
[2]U.S. Department of Commerce income account data also shows that the rate of
savings in Hawaii has been considerably above the U.S. average.
[3]There could be other perhaps more satisfactory definitions of discretionary
income per household, but we have constructed our definition to conform to data
available. This data should be accepted with some reservations, because the city
of Honolulu includes high income suburban type areas, whereas the higher income
suburbs are not a part of many of the cities surveyed.

travel similar to direct relationship between the rate of travel and family income level.[4] It also showed that families with an income of $6,000 or more do most of the traveling in the country. This data and other data indicate that non-business travel is quite income elastic. As income increases, the per cent spent on vacation and other non-business travel increases more sharply. Moreover, families with higher incomes have a higher propensity to travel and spend a higher proportion of their income on travel. On the basis of fairly high average family income, discretionary income, and rate of savings, and the relatively rapid growth in personal incomes, there seems to be a potential for increased travel by Island residents.

Consumer preferences and vacation habits.--The 1963 Census of Transportation shows substantial travel by Americans. The American public completed 257 million trips involving 487 million travelers who spent more than 2 billion nights away from home.[5] Well over four-fifths of the trips were by automobile. More than two-thirds of the travelers were in parties of two or more persons. About three out of five trips were to visit relatives and friends and for pleasure. Over half of the trips were for a distance of over 100 miles and for three days or longer. About one-sixth of the trips were for a week or longer.

From available evidence, people in Hawaii tend to travel less than the average on the mainland. We do not say that we can expect Hawaiian residents to travel the equivalent of Mainland residents or that national travel patterns are relevant for the state. Hawaiian residents differ in many ways, including habits, racial characteristics, culture, ways of recreation, and mode of living. Moreover, the isolation of the islands and the sea between them have been among the barriers to travel.

---

[4]Bureau of Census, 1963 Census of Transportation, National Travel, November, 1964, p. 1 and p. 9.

[5]See 1963 Census of Transportation, National Travel, op. cit. p. 1.

82

Since the previous sea ferry terminated its service, practically all inter-island travel has been by the two airlines. As Table III-10 in the Appendix to this chapter shows, inter-island air travel by state residents has increased slowly, while there has been a sharp increase in air travel by out-of-state visitors during the last decade. Air trips by out-of-state visitors have increased at an average annual rate of about 17 per cent from 1953 to 1963 compared to about 3 per cent for state residents. Thus, inter-island travel by Hawaiian residents has been growing fairly slowly.

Since state residents have only had air travel available for more than a decade, they have developed a habit to travel by air. In both our surveys of households and shippers, many people expressed a preference for travel by air, especially because of speed and convenience. Thus, considerable consumer preference probably exists for inter-island air travel. Still, as our survey of households and all previous surveys indicate, there is a widespread aspiration of the people of the state for a lower cost, alternative means of inter-island transportation.

The differences in travel patterns of Hawaii residents and those on the mainland, therefore, may be related in part to opportunities available. Mainland residents have a network of highways that give them a great variety of opportunities for travel. They also usually have a number of alternative ways of traveling, including railroad, bus, and airlines. Hawaiian residents, on the other hand, have only the airlines available for inter-island travel. While it is not feasible, what would be travel by state residents, if major highways connected all the major islands?

Another aspect of the problem is the scenic and recreational attractions the other islands offer to residents of Oahu to induce them to go repeatedly to the other islands. It is well known that there are major scenic attractions on

the neighbor islands. But many things may have to be done to encourage large numbers of people to go to the neighbor islands repeatedly. This includes construction or improvement of highways, cabins, beaches, and other recreational areas.

Still, even if all these aspects of a system to encourage inter-island travel are undertaken, the opportunities available to state residents will not be the equivalent of opportunities available to mainland residents to travel by automobile, bus, train, and plane to a great variety of scenic and recreational areas. Moreover, island residents tend to have a high propensity to travel to the mainland and foreign countries.

Cost of travel.--Another key factor in passenger demand for an inter-island ferry service is the cost of travel. Cost includes not only the fares but also the expenses of staying and traveling on the other islands. A recent report by Professor Mund shows that the Hawaiian air fares per mile in many cases are above the average for local carriers for similar distances on the mainland.[6] However, the differences become less significant when one considers the family fare plan rates, which are available during specified hours.

More significant than the air fares is the fact that people on the mainland usually have several alternatives, lower cost, means of travel available, including automobile, bus, and train. Of special importance, is the possibility to travel by automobile, which involves convenience and lower out-of-pocket costs, especially for families and groups.

Another aspect of travel to the neighbor islands are the high costs of lodging, food, and car rentals for a vacation trip. Visitors to the neighbor islands do not have a wide range of moderately-priced hotels and restaurants

---

[6]Mund, Vernon A., Competition and Regulation of Air Transportation in Hawaii, Economic Research Center, University of Hawaii, 1965. Differences in air fares may be explained by comparative load factors, schedules, costs of operation and other factors.

available like in Honolulu or most areas on the mainland. For the most part, the comfortable hotels are usually first class or luxury hotels for tourists. Most of the good restaurants are located at these hotels. Even at Kamaaina rates, the costs are high for lodging and meals at these hotels. While car rentals are reasonable on a per day basis, they become expensive for a stay of several days, a week, or longer. Thus, the combination of air fares and the costs of staying and traveling on the neighbor islands make vacations there expensive, unless people stay with relatives or friends.

The establishment of an inter-island ferry system would not only provide an alternative, lower cost means of transportation for travel by people with automobiles, but it should also encourage development of lower cost facilities to serve visitors. It should lead to investments in moderately-priced hotels, motels, restaurants, and other establishments to serve visitors. Presumably, the state would construct cabins, which would make available lower price accommodations for families. Thus, the whole structure of costs of trips to the neighbor islands could be changed. Passenger demand should be considered not in terms of current costs of travel and facilities available but in terms of a possibly new structure induced by an inter-island ferry system.

Seasonal aspects.--From our survey and other information available, passenger demand for travel on a ferry is likely to be quite seasonal. According to our survey during the year prior to the interviews, as much as 49 per cent of pleasure household trips were made during the three summer months of June, July and August. We can expect a similar pattern of demand for family pleasure travel on a ferry. Demand is also likely to be concentrated on weekends, especially longer weekends.

One way of dealing with this problem is through a rate structure with higher rates during the months of June to August and at peak holiday periods and lower rates during the rest of the year. There could also be somewhat higher rates on

weekends and lower rates during the weekdays. Special group rates could be provided during the off-season and for week day trips. Tourist travel and group travel by ferry could be vigorously promoted during the off season periods. Furthermore, there are some tendencies for people in Hawaii as on the mainland to take all or part of vacations at periods other than the summer months.

Comfortable trips and efficient service.--In the last analysis, a major key to passenger demand for a ferry service is comfortable and attractive ocean voyages between the islands. Our household survey and our demand analysis are based upon a possible sea ferry providing comfortable trips and efficient service to passengers. Marine architects believe that ocean-going ferries can be designed that will offer passengers reasonbly comfortable trips over the seas between the islands. Ferry systems have been operated successfully in other parts of the world, such as Australia and Europe, where there are rough seas comparable to the waters around Hawaii. Finally, if the boat trips are comfortable, facilities such as restaurants, a cocktail lounge, bar, movies, other lounges, observation desks and comfortable seats can make sea ferry trips enjoyable.

In summary, this brief examination of per capita income, family income, discretionary family income, recent growth in incomes, vacation travel in the United States, consumption patterns in Hawaii, and the impact of a possible ferry on costs of vacations, tend to reinforce the results from the survey of households. All this analysis is based upon a possible ferry service providing people with automobiles comfortable and efficient service.

APPENDIX TO CHAPTER III

TABLE III-7

PER CAPITA PERSONAL AND DISPOSABLE INCOME FOR HAWAII AND THE UNITED STATES

	Per Capita Personal Income Hawaii	Per Cent Increase from Previous Year	Per Capita Personal Income United States	Per Cent Increase from Previous Year	Per Capita Disposable Personal Income Hawaii	U.S.A.
1950	$1,403		$1,491		1,267	1,354
1951	1,589	13.3	1,649	10.6		
1952	1,745	9.8	1,727	4.7		
1953	1,782	2.1	1,788	3.5	1,569	1,565
1954	1,768	0.8	1,770	1.0		
1955	1,789	1.2	1,866	5.4	1,600	1,651
1956	1,862	4.1	1,975	5.8		
1957	1,916	2.9	2,048	3.7	1,677	1,800
1958	1,946	1.6	2,064	0.8		
1959	2,118	8.8	2,163	4.8	1,842	1,900
1960	2,274	7.4	2,217	2.5		
1961	2,358	3.7	2,268	2.3	1,997	1,981
1962	2,394	1.5	2,368	4.4		
1963	2,493	4.1	2,449	3.4	2,097	2,123

Source: Survey of Current Business, August, 1964, U.S. Department of Commerce.

Note: Per capita income for Hawaii in 1963 estimate by First National Bank of Hawaii, which is slightly higher than prior estimate of $2,462 in survey of current business.

TABLE III-7

PER CAPITA PERSONAL AND DISPOSABLE
INCOME FOR HAWAII AND THE UNITED STATES

Year	Per Capita Personal Income Hawaii	Per Cent Increase from Previous Year	Per Capita Personal Income United States	Per Cent Increase from Previous Year	Per Capita Disposable Personal Income Hawaii	Per Cent Increase from Previous Year	U.S.A.
1950	$1,403		$1,491			$1,267	1,354
1951	1,589	13.3	1,649	10.6			
1952	1,745	9.8	1,722	4.7	1,509		1,565
1953	1,782	2.1	1,788	3.5	1,569		1,565
1954	1,788	0.8	1,770	1.0			1,651
1955	1,789	1.2	1,866	5.4	1,600		1,651
1956	1,882	6.1	1,975	5.8			1,706
1957	1,916	2.9	2,048	3.7	1,677		1,800
1958	1,966	1.9	2,066	0.8			1,900
1959	2,116	8.8	2,165	4.8	1,807		1,900
1960	2,271	7.4	2,177	2.5			1,981
1961	2,358	3.7	2,266	2.3	1,997		1,981
1962	2,394	1.5	2,368	4.4			2,123
1963	2,493	4.1	2,469				

SOURCE: Survey of Current Business, August, 1964, U.S. Department of Commerce.

Note: Per capita income for Hawaii in 1963 is an estimate of First National Bank of Hawaii, which is slightly higher than prior estimate of $2,482 in Survey of Current Business.

88

TABLE III-8

HAWAII'S RANK AMONG THE 50 STATES IN KEY INCOME AND OTHER FACTORS, 1963

	Hawaii	United States	Rank of Hawaii among States
Personal income per capita	$2,476	$2,443	16
Median family income	7,680	7,140	8
Per cent of low income family (under $3,000)	12.9	21.4	45
Per cent of families with income $10,000 or higher	22.0	15.1	2
Per cent urban population	76.5	69.9	
Median school years completed	11.3	10.6	17

Source: Bank of Hawaii, Annual Economic Report, 1964.

-198-

TABLE III-8

HAWAII'S RANK AMONG THE 50 STATES IN KEY INCOME AND OTHER FACTORS, 1963

	Hawaii	United States	Rank of Hawaii among 50 states
Personal income per capita	$2,676	$2,443	16
Median family income	7,560	6,160	8
Per cent of low income family (under $3,000)	12.9	21.4	45-5
Per cent of families with income $10,000 or higher	22.0	15.1	3
Per cent urban population	76.5	69.9	
Median school years completed	11.7	10.6	17

Source: Bank of Hawaii, Annual Economic Report, 1964.

89

TABLE III-9

ESTIMATES DISCRETIONARY INCOME PER HOUSEHOLD IN HONOLULU, 1961

	Hawaii	United States	Net Per Cent Difference Hawaii/U.S.	Major Regions			
				West	North Central	South	Northeast
Money income after taxes	$7,950	$5,957	33.5%	$6,386	$5,863	$5,036	$6,604
Add: other money receipts	169	93	81.7	52	103	86	116
Total money income	8,119	6,050	34.2	6,438	5,966	5,122	6,720
Deduct: necessary consumption and other obligations	5,348	4,588	16.6	4,699	4,462	3,931	5,218
Food prepared at home	1,308	1,034	26.5	1,025	1,015	848	1,220
Housing, total	1,729	1,585	9.1	1,648	1,540	1,327	1,818
Fuel, light, refrigeration, water	196	248	(21.0)	213	256	219	285
Household operations	333	317	20.8	333	291	292	356
Clothing	577	563	2.5	566	541	486	649
Medical care	403	362	11.3	420	346	322	379
Personal care	207	156	32.7	156	151	154	162
Personal insurance	545	323	68.7	338	322	283	349
Discretionary income per household	2,771	1,462	89.5	1,739	1,504	1,191	1,502

Source: Harry T. Oshima and Mitsuo Ono, Hawaii's Income and Expenditures, 1958, 1959, and 1960, Vol. II, Economic Research Center, January, 1965, pp. V-23 and V-24.

90

TABLE III-10

INTER-ISLAND AIR TRIPS (1951-63 calendar years)
(Number of enplanements in thousands)

	Total	Out of State Visitors	Hawaiian Residents	Per Cent Out of State	Per Cent Hawaiian Residents
1951	490	78	412	16	84
1952	546	93	453	17	83
1953	562	124	438	22	78
1954	565	147	418	26	74
1955	619	186	433	30	70
1956	640	211	429	33	67
1957	674	256	418	38	62
1958	636	210	426	33	67
1959	820	320	500	3 9	61
1960	966	406	560	42	58
1961	939	394	545	42	58
1962	980	461	519	47	53
1963	1,144	561	583	49	51

Note: For 1962-1963 percentages vary between 50-53 per cent for Hawaiian residents, HAL estimates.

Source: Hawaii State Department of Transportation, Airport Division for Total Enplanements, M. Stuart, Some Trends in the Honolulu Outer-Island Air Passenger Traffic Pattern of Hawaiian Islands, 1951-1961: A Geographic Case Study, typed master thesis, University of Hawaii, June 1963, for percentage estimates 1951-61.

TABLE III-10.

HULA-GRASS/AIRPORT TOURS (1951-63 calendar years)
(Number of organizations in thousands)

Year	Total	Out of State Visitors	Hawaiian Residents	Per Cent Out of State	Per Cent Waikiki for Residents
1951	490	78	412	16	84
1952	546	95	452	17	83
1953	502	114	453	23	75
1954	565	147	413	26	74
1955	615	185	430	30	70
1956	640	217	412	32	68
1957	574	256	318	38	62
1958	636	210	426	33	67
1959	570	270	300	39	61
1960	556	406	560	42	58
1961	735	304	565	42	58
1962	905	463	515	47	53
1963	1,164	561	564	49	51

Note: For 1953-1963 percentages vary between 50-85 per cent for Hawaiian residents, H/T estimates.

Source: Hawaii State Department of Transportation, Airport Division for hotel employments. M. Stuart, Some Trends in the Honolulu Oahu-Inbound Air Passenger Traffic Pattern of Hawaiian Islands, 1951-1961, unpublished thesis, University of Hawaii, June 1963, for per cent Oahu resident (1951-61).

CHAPTER IV

COST ESTIMATES FOR THE PROPOSED FERRY SYSTEM

In our discussion we shall briefly examine capital costs of constructing two ships and necessary harbor and terminal facilities. Then we shall examine annual cost, including debt service, operation and maintenance of ships and terminals, and administration costs.

Our analysis of costs starts with the estimates made in the Law and Wilson-Tudor study, which as we previously indicated made the most comprehensive study of the physical aspects of a surface ferry and the costs involved. While we have used the costs estimates in the Law and Wilson-Tudor report as a starting point, we have re-examined each of the cost items and recalculated many of them, utilizing the most expert advice available within the restrictions imposed by time. For example, we have used information provided by Eastman Dillon, Union Securities & Co., the State Finance Division, and security analysis on a state bond issue, and servicing costs. The Harbors Division furnished us with a number of estimates of cost of terminals and harbor construction. We received some judgments on possible rises in costs of building and operating ships and on administrative expenses from the Harbors Division and other maritime interests. We checked minimum crew requirements with the Coast Guard. Union leaders gave us copies of union contracts with the Alaska Ferry System. We checked the costs of personal fuel, ships stores, repairs, maintenance and drydocking with engineering and operating personnel of steamship companies. We consulted insurance underwriters on the costs of maritime insurance. We also received some data on costs of operation from the Alaska Ferry System and talked to the former Director of Economic Development and Planning of Alaska when he was in Honolulu.

We should emphasize that our cost estimates are tentative for the purpose of estimating possible deficits. We do not say that these costs will be realized;

we have found that actual costs often exceed preliminary estimates. There are too many unpredictable elements to estimate costs in any precise fashion at this point. If the state decides to operate a ferry and definite decisions are made on the type of bond issue and terms, the type of ships, terminal facilities, necessary harbor construction which the state may have to finance, routes and schedules and other factors, and contracts are negotiated with the unions involved, then precise cost estimates can be made. It should also be emphasized that the bond issues actually issued by the State of Alaska for its ferry system and the costs of building ships and operating them substantially exceeded estimates made in earlier studies.

These cost estimates are based on the type of ferry operation briefly described in Chapter II. In summary this would involve ocean-going vessels with an overall length of about 370 feet, a sustained speed of 18 knots, fin stabilizers or flume tanks, bow steering and the most modern technical characteristics available at reasonable cost. The ships would be capable of carrying about 500 passengers and 106 regular size automobiles or 52 highway trailers. The exact details of the schedule would have to be worked out, but we assume practically daily service to the major islands. The trips would be on the leeward side between Honolulu and Kaunakakai on Molokai, Maalaea on Maui, Kawaihae on Hawaii; however, some trips would go to Hilo instead of Kawaihae on Hawaii. Service between Honolulu and Nawiliwili on Kauai would be about five times a week.

If the state legislature approves a ferry system during the 1965 session, we assume that construction of ships and port facilities would commence in 1966 and would be completed sometime in 1968, and the ferry system could start operations in 1969.

We are making two cost estimates, lower and higher estimates under carefully elaborated conditions. Actually, we recognize that there are many possible estimates

under different assumptions. Our lower and higher cost estimates are neither
minimum nor maximum estimates, but rather a range under the conditions stated.
Any change in the design of ships, and port facilities, the routes served, service
provided, and other key factors in a ferry operation would mean that the cost
estimates would have to be revised.

1. Capital Investments

Vessels.--The most comprehensive analysis of a suitable ship design for
inter-island ferry and the costs of construction were made in the Preferred Water
Ferry Plan of the Law and Wilson-Tudor report. Without going into technical
details, this report recommended two identical ships with the following characteristics: an overall length of 371 feet, length at waterline of 344 feet, beam of
72 feet, draft of 15 feet, displacement of 3,900 long tons, shaft horsepower of
8,000, speed of 18 knots, fin stabilizers, bow steering, passenger capacity of
500 persons, and vehicle capacity of 106 automobiles or 52 highway trailers.
The vessel as described would have four decks with ample accommodations for
passengers, including observation decks, a restaurant, a cocktail lounge, some
staterooms, and adequate accomodations for crew.

We recognize that if a decision is made to operate a ferry, there could very
well be modifications in the final design to incorporate the most modern aspects
of technology available. For example, some marine architects propose flume tanks
instead of fin stabilizers. Also, an engineer with Matson Lines suggested that
the vessels should be sand blasted and demet coated, in order to reduce maintenance
costs. Furthermore, as suggested in the Guralnick paper, some of the so-called
frills might be eliminated, such as staterooms and cocktail lounges and greater
use might be made of airplane type of seats in order to keep costs down. In these
types of decisions, any possible reductions of costs have to be considered against
passenger comfort and a possible adverse impact on demand.

94

The Law and Wilson-Tudor report estimated that the type of ships that they recommended could be constructed for approximately $6,000,000, based upon completion of the ships at the end of 1963. The Coverdale and Colpitts report completed in January 1964, indicated that this type of ferry ship could be constructed at a cost of $6,000,000 by the end of 1967. In considering the ferry issue in the 1964 session, the state legislature also assumed that each ship could be built for not more than $6,000,000. However, in the case of the Alaska Ferry System, the actual costs of constructing ships exceeded original estimates, partly because of changes in design.

Engineers at the Harbors Division were inclined to believe that each ship could still be built for about $6,000,000, but they did not profess to be experts in this matter. However, we recognize that shipbuilding costs have been rising, and it is considered to be prudent to allow about three per cent for an increase in costs.[1] On the other hand, there is the possibility that some changes in design, such as greater simplicity and elimination of so-called frills such as staterooms and cocktail lounges could offset increases in costs and keep construction cost at $6,000,000 or less per ship. Therefore, we have two estimates, a lower one of $6,000,000 per ship and a higher one of about $6,600,000 per ship based upon a ten per cent increase in costs and completion of the construction of the ships in 1968.

Terminal facilities and harbor construction.--There are a number of estimates available on the costs of terminal facilities and harbor improvement, including those in the Law and Wilson-Tudor and Coverdale and Colpitts reports. Obviously, the costs of terminal and harbor facilities depend on the type of ship, the routes and ports used, the method of loading and unloading automobiles, the method of handling, and the extent of shipping freight among other things.

---

[1]For the sake of simplicity, we provide for a ten per cent increase in the cost of building the ships from 1965 to 1968 in our higher estimate.

95

Our analysis, as has been mentioned previously, is based on a ferry system primarily handling passengers and automobiles, with limited handling of cargo on a roll-on, roll-off basis. Without going into technical details, an essential requirement in this type of operation is minimum loading and unloading time and rapid turn-around and departure. Since cargo is expected to be supplementary in this kind of operation, we do not make any provision for special loading facilities for cargo.

In view of some changes in routes and also differences in the concept of a ferry, especially less emphasis on cargo handling, the Law and Wilson-Tudor estimates of about three million dollars for terminal facilities seem to be out-moded. In fact, staff members of the Harbors Division stated that a ferry operation could be undertaken with less elaborate facilities.[2] The Coverdale and Colpitts report, as shown in Table IV-1, used minimum terminal facilities costing a total of $795,000, provided by the Harbors Division in 1963. However, these estimates are not relevant because they provide for a ferry going on the windward side over longer distances and rough seas to Kahului and Hilo; they omit Kaunakakai on Molokai entirely. They do not provide for any harbor improvements.

The Harbors Division has a number of estimates of costs of terminals. Recently staff members of the division furnished new estimates of costs of terminal facilities at Maalaea, Kawaihae, and Nawiliwili based on the latest thinking about a ferry operation. We recognize that any estimates are highly tentative at this time. In Table IV-1 we show various cost estimates made in previous reports and the ones recently made by the Harbors Division.

As our lower cost estimates for terminal facilities, we are using minimum estimates available. For Honolulu we are using the estimates for terminals on the

---

[2] Mr. Melvin Lepine, Chief of the Harbors Division, and members of his staff were very helpful in providing information about costs of terminal facilities and harbor construction.

96

TABLE IV-1

VARIOUS ESTIMATES OF COSTS OF TERMINALS AND HARBOR CONSTRUCTION
FOR A FERRY SYSTEM
(Thousands of Dollars)

| | Law and Wilson-Tudor Report[1] | | Terminals | | |
| | | | Minimum Estimates Coverdale & Colpitts Report[2] | More Recent Estimates State Harbors Division[3] | Estimates for Harbor Construction[4] |
	Terminal Facilities	Harbor Construction			
Honolulu, Oahu	450		150-230		
Nawiliwili, Kauai	270		210	330	67
Kaunakakai, Molokai	225	1,455			1,836
Maalaea, Maui				448	1,418
Lahaina, Maui	215	2,155			
Kahului, Maui	445		210		
Kawaihae, Hawaii	390		85	478	244
Hilo, Hawaii	565		140		
Totals or Sub-totals	2,560	3,610	795-875	1,256	3,565
Contract Administration and Engineering	505	325			
Total	3,065 +	3,935			
GRAND TOTAL	7,000				

[1] The Law and Wilson-Tudor report made estimates of terminal and harbor construction for Lahaina, rather than Maalaea.

[2] Minimum estimates for terminal facilities prepared by Harbors Division, State Department of Transportation, for Coverdale and Colpitts, in letter of October 17, 1963. Amounts in this table are for side port and stern loading. Two estimates are shown for Honolulu. The lower estimate of $150,000 is based on use of Pier 7 (Waikiki or east side), which would present some serious traffic problems. The higher estimate for Honolulu is based on use of the Waikiki side of Pier 5-6 alongside the proposed parking lot. This higher estimate may be more realistic. Coverdale and Colpitts used the lower estimate of $795,000 in its report.

97

TABLE IV-1--Continued

3/More recent estimates were prepared by the Harbors Division, State Department of Transportation, based on the latest thinking.

4/Estimates for harbor construction are based on Corps of Engineers projects for Kaunakakai and Maalaea. The other estimates consist of necessary dredging as estimated by the Harbors Division, State Department of Transportation. The necessary harbor construction for a ferry operation for Maalaea and Kaunakakai might vary from these amounts.

Sources: Law and Wilson-Tudor, State of Hawaii Transportation Plan, p. 110 and Hawaii Department of Transportation, Harbors Division, files.

98

Waikiki side of piers 5 and 6, which would create less of a traffic problem than other locations. We are providing a 10 per cent contingency of increased costs for construction. Our estimates are shown in Table IV-2. Our lower cost estimate assumes that the state would not have to pay for any necessary harbor construction.

A ferry system going to the ports that we have designated will also require major harbor improvement of Maalaea and Kaunakakai and dredging at Kawaihae and Nawiliwili. The Law and Wilson-Tudor report considered harbor construction costs, but seems to be out-of-date, partly because of changes in the proposed port from Lahaina to Maalaea on Maui.

The major part or all costs of harbor construction could be borne by the federal government, providing the required projects are approved by the Corps of Engineers and then are submitted to Congress for approval, and the appropriations are provided by the Congress of the United States. But this can be a time-consuming process.

At the present time a project has been approved by Congress for harbor construction at Kaunakakai, Molokai; however, work has not started as it is conditional on the establishment of a cannery on the island. According to the Harbors Division, this harbor construction would be adequate to handle the ferry ships. There are no present indications that the cannery is going to be established on Molokai. But it may be possible to justify implementation of the project, if the inter-island ferry system is approved.

A project for harbor construction at Maalaea, Maui, has been submitted for Congressional action through the Corps of Engineers.[3] The project, however, does not provide necessary facilities for the operation of a ferry system. It would have to be revised to make the harbor suitable to handle ocean-going ferries. If a ferry is approved by the state legislature, it is conceivable that the project

---

[3] Another project has been submitted to Congress for harbor improvement at Lahaina, Maui. This project also makes no provision for harbor facilities for a ferry operation.

99

TABLE IV-2

ESTIMATED COSTS OF TERMINALS AND HARBOR IMPROVEMENTS
(Thousands of Dollars)

	Minimum Estimates Available for Terminals[1]	More Recent or Higher Estimates Terminals[2]	Harbor Construction Including Dredging[3]
Honolulu, Oahu	230	276	
Nawiliwili, Kauai	210	330	67
Kaunakakai, Molokai	225	270	1,836
Maalaea, Maui	448	448	1,418
Kawaihae, Hawaii	85	478	244
Hilo, Hawaii	140	168	
Sub-total	1,338	1,970	3,565
10 per cent contingency for increase in costs	134	197	357
TOTAL	1,472	2,167	3,922

[1] Minimum estimates are based on those furnished to Coverdale & Colpitts by the Harbors Division, State Department of Transportation, and other minimum estimates available. Estimates for Honolulu are based on using the Waikiki side of Piers 5 and 6, which is considered to be more realistic.

[2] Higher estimates are based upon using latest estimates provided by the Harbors Division, Department of Transportation, for the ports of Nawiliwili, Maalaea, and Kawaihae. The estimates for the other ports are the minimum estimates increased by 20 per cent as they were considered to be low. These estimates should by no means be considered as maximum estimates.

[3] See Table IV-1.

TABLE IV-2

ESTIMATED COSTS OF TERMINALS AND HARBOR IMPROVEMENTS
(Thousands of Dollars)

	Minimum Estimates Available for Terminals[1]	More Recent or Higher Estimates[2]	Harbor Construction Including Dredging[3]
Honolulu, Oahu	210	276	
Nawiliwili, Kauai	210	330	67
Kaunakakai, Molokai	225	170	1,836
Kahului, Maui	468	468	1,416
Kawaihae, Hawaii	85	378	246
Hilo, Hawaii	140	108	
Sub-total	1,338	1,870	3,563
10 per cent contingency for increase in costs	134	187	359
TOTAL	1,472	2,057	3,922

Source: Table IV-1.

[1] Minimum estimates are based on those submitted to Governor's Committee on ___ by the Harbors Division, State Department of Transportation, and other minimum estimates available. Estimates for Honolulu are based on using the Waikiki side of Piers 5 and 6, which is considered to be more realistic.

[2] Higher estimates are based upon inflationist estimates provided by the Harbors Division, Department of Transportation, for the ports of Nawiliwili, Kahului and Kawaihae. The estimates for the other ports are the minimum estimates increased by 20 per cent as they were considered to be low. These estimates should by no means be considered as maximum estimates.

could be revised through the Corps of Engineers for Congressional action. Whether this could be done in time for Congressional action in 1965 is dubious. It would require much speedier action at all levels than is customary in such matters. Perhaps the Hawaiian Congressional delegation could help to speed up action. The alternative would be to have a special act by Congress to enable the State of Hawaii to start harbor construction and be reimbursed after the project is approved through the usual procedures. We also have to consider that considerable time is involved in contracting and implementing federal harbor projects.

Thus, the question of the federal government assuming the costs of necessary harbor construction or improvement required for the ferry at Maalaea, Kaunakakai, Kawaihae, and Nawiliwili is a complex and uncertain one. It involves the time of commencement of a ferry operation if it is approved by the state. Would the state be willing, if necessary, to delay the start of a ferry operation to obtain federal funds for necessary harbor construction? How long would it take to have projects revised or approved through normal procedures and have appropriations voted by Congress? How long would it take to have harbor construction projects completed under federal appropriations? Can the political process and the implementation be speeded up to meet plans of the state in a possible ferry operation? Can a special law be passed by Congress enabling the state government to go ahead and be reimbursed later? There are no clear answers to these questions. Nevertheless, if the state decides to put a ferry system into operation, it would be worthwhile for the state to investigate with the Congressional delegation all possibilities of obtaining federal funds for necessary harbor improvement in view of the large expenditures involved.

In our analysis our higher estimate is based on an assumption that the state will have to pay for the costs of harbor construction; that is, it will not be possible to obtain the necessary federal funds rapidly enough. The higher estimate

is also based on higher costs of construction of terminals; it uses the more recent estimates provided by the Harbors Division for the ports of Maalaea, Nawiliwili, and Kawaihae. Once again we have a 10 per cent contingency for an increase in construction costs. Both the higher and lower estimates for port facilities are shown in Table IV-2.

In Table IV-3 the lower and higher estimates of capital costs, including ships and port facilities are summarized. The lower capital cost estimate is $13,472,000 while the higher one is $19,289,000. We should emphasize that these capital costs do not include costs of cabins and highways, which would probably be required in conjunction with a ferry system.

TABLE IV-3

LOWER AND HIGHER ESTIMATES OF CAPITAL COSTS

	Thousands of Dollars
Lower Cost Estimate	
Two ships	12,000
Terminal facilities	1,472
Total	13,472
Higher Cost Estimate	
Two ships	13,200
Terminal facilities	2,167
Harbor construction	3,922
Total	19,289

2. Annual Costs

Bond issue and servicing costs.--The major fixed burden that has to be met is the annual debt service requirements, including interest and amortization of bond principal. From the standpoint of economics or accounting, amortization of bond principal is not a cost but rather a repayment of debt. What would be a cost is depreciation on ships and terminal and harbor facilities. However, from the standpoint of financial analysis a key factor would be the annual fixed charges that would have to be met to service the bond issue. The amortization of debt may be considered roughly the equivalent of depreciation, as long as the term of the bond issue is about equivalent to the estimated life of the capital investments, in this case the ferry ships and port facilities.

The debt service charges would depend upon the type of state bonds issued, the principal of the bonds, their maturities, the interest rates on them, the provisions for sinking fund and repayment, and many other factors. The amount of bonds would have to provide adequate funds for the capital investments; they might also have to provide funds for payment of net interest on bonds until the ferry goes into operation, and for any costs of financing the bond issue.[4]

The state government has a choice of issuing general obligation bonds at a lower rate of interest or revenue bonds at a higher rate of interest. Past consideration in the state legislature has been primarily based on a revenue bond issue. However, in this session the state legislature is considering bills providing for general obligation bonds as well as revenue bonds. The main advantage of general obligation bonds--and an important one--is lower interest rates. On the other hand, there has been considerable support for a revenue bond issue, because of limits on the state debt, which apply to general obligation but not to revenue bonds.

_____

[4]The bond issue might also have to provide some working capital and some funds for contingencies. However, we are assuming the state government can advance initial working capital funds until bonds are sold.

103

According to a letter received early in 1964 from Eastman Dillon, Union Securities & Company, a revenue bond issue is feasible if (a) the state establishes minimum rates and charges to assure that revenues will be at least sufficient to provide for annual debt service requirements and (b) the state unconditionally guarantees to operate the ferry system and collect rates so long as any bonds shall be outstanding.[5]

While most recent consideration of a ferry system has been based on revenue bonds, some state legislators have proposed a plan for general obligation bonds that would be feasible within the existing debt limit. Therefore, in our lower cost estimate we are assuming general obligation bonds, while in our higher estimate we are assuming revenue bonds with the above stipulations.

In checking with the State Finance Division, we find that it has been using an interest rate of 3.4 per cent for purposes of projections for the next year on general obligation bonds with a term of 20 years, although actual interest rates have recently been lower than that.[6] For general obligation bonds for 25 or 30 years the interest rates would be higher. In our lower cost estimate we consider general obligation bonds for 25 years at 3.5 per cent interest as reasonable. We also assume that the state will issue general obligation bonds about two years before commencement of the ferry operation, that half of the funds can be reinvested at 3 per cent interest, and that amortization of

[5]Letter from Eastman Dillon, Union Securities & Company, addressed to Dr. Fujio Matsuda, Director, Department of Transportation, State of Hawaii, dated January 15, 1964.

[6]Mr. Howard H. Adams of the State Finance Division was very helpful in providing information on general obligation bond issues, including current and planning interest rates. He also provided information on some current interest rates on revenue bonds.

bond principal will start the first year of the ferry operation, i.e., 1969.[7]

The bond principal includes capitalized net interest for an interim period of

two years. On this basis as shown in Table IV-4 the amount of bond principal

would be $14,052,000, and the annual debt service charges would be about $900,000

over 23 years.[8]

With respect to our higher cost estimate we have tried to ascertain

realistic interest rates on revenue bonds. In its letter early in 1964, Eastman

Dillon, Union Securities & Co. estimated an interest rate of 5 per cent on

revenue bonds for a ferry system, based on passenger fares of 70 per cent of

airline rates and 5.5 per cent based on Hulten Committee suggested fares. The

actual interest rates, of course, would depend on market conditions at the time

of the bond sale and the capital market's evaluation of risk and other factors.

We have checked interest rates on a possible revenue issue at this time

(March, 1965) with an official of the State Finance Division and an investment

analyst. We have received a range of estimated interest rates from 5 to 5.5

per cent. In our higher cost estimate, we are using an interest rate of 5

per cent on revenue bonds in view of a more favorable revenue projection.

Along the lines suggested by Eastman Dillon, Union Securities & Co,

---

[7]Actually, the bonds could be sold in series as funds are required to meet expenditures for ships and terminals. This would involve some savings on interest costs. However, we have not been able to obtain any definite information on the timing of fund requirements. Our assumption on sale of bonds and reinvestment of part of the funds is similar to that of Eastman Dillon, Union Securities & Co. in their letter of January, 1965.

[8]On the other hand, we could assume that the state legislature would make appropriations for interest charges on general obligation bonds until a ferry goes into operation. In that case the principal of the bonds would be about $13,472,000 and the annual debt service would be about $862,000 over 23 years. This might be more normal procedure. However, in our calculations we want our estimates to include the full cost of a ferry operation. We do not want to hide some costs by assuming appropriations by the legislature.

TABLE IV-4

LOWER AND HIGHER ESTIMATES OF AMOUNT OF BOND ISSUES AND ANNUAL DEBT SERVICE[1]

		Thousands of Dollars
Lower Cost Estimate - General Obligation Bonds		
Costs of 2 ships		12,000
Costs of terminals		1,472
Capital costs		13,472
Capitalized interest 2 years at 3.5%	984	
Less: Interest earned at 3%	404	580
Principal of bonds		14,052
Debt service charges per year for 23 years		900
Higher Cost Estimate - Revenue Bonds		
Costs of 2 ships		13,200
Costs of terminals		2,167
Harbor construction		3,922
Total capital costs		19,289
Capitalized interest 2 years at 5%	2,150	
Less: Interest earned at 3%	578	1,572
Financing and other expenses		645
Principal of bonds		21,506
Debt service charges per year for 28 years		1,443

[1] The procedures used to estimate the principal of bond issues are similar to those used by Eastman Dillon, Union Securities & Co. in its letter of January, 1964, to Dr. Matsuda, Director of Transportation. The general obligation bonds do not provide any financing costs, as Mr. Adams of the State Finance Office indicated that they are minor. The revenue bonds provide about 3 per cent of bond principal for financing costs and possible discounts.

TABLE IV-4

TOTAL AND ANNUAL ESTIMATED COST OF VARIOUS PORT ISSUES AND ANNUAL DEBT SERVICE[1/]

Thousands
of Dollars

Lower Cost Estimate - General-Obligation bonds

Costs of 2 ships		12,000
Costs of terminals		1,411
Capital costs		13,411
Capitalized interest 2 years at 3.5%	926	
Less: Interest earned at 3%	406	580
Proceeds of bonds		14,077
Debt service charges per year for 40 years		900

Higher Cost Estimate - Revenue bonds

Costs of 2 ships		15,200
Costs of terminals		2,167
Harbor construction		1,922
Total capital costs		19,289
Capitalized interest 2 years at 5%	2,150	
Less: Interest earned at 5%	378	1,772
Financing and other expenses		645
Principal of bonds		21,706
Debt service charge per year for 30 years		1,643

1/ The procedures used to estimate the principal of bond issues are similar to those used by Eastman Dillon, Union Securities & Co. in its letter of January, 1962, to Mr. Matsuda, Director of Transportation. The general obligation bonds do not provide any financing margin as 5%. Bonds of the State Finance Office indicated that they are exempt. The revenue bonds provide about a 5 per cent of bond principal for financing costs and possible discounts.

we are also assuming that a revenue bond issue is feasible for 30 years. The
Law and Wilson-Tudor report suggested two separate bond issues, a 25 year-
issue for the capital costs of ships and a 30-year issue for terminal and
harbor facilities, based on a 25-year normal life of ships and a longer life
for port facilities. Other estimates of the life of ships range from 20 to 30
years, although maritime authorities say that it is possible to operate them
for 30 years or longer. We accept the evaluation of Eastman Dillon, Union
Securities & Co. that 30 years is an appropriate term for a ferry issue,
although we recognize that the term might have to be reduced to 25 years after
further investment analysis.

There are many possible ways for providing amortization of bond principal
in a revenue issue, including serial maturities, mandatory sinking fund payments,
or a combination of both. The exact provisions would have to be worked out with
investment underwriters and are beyond the scope of this report. For the
purpose of making estimates of annual debt service requirements, we are assuming
that the bonds would be sold on an average of two years before the ferry goes
into operation; they would have a maturity of 30 years; mandatory sinking fund
payments would start the first year of the ferry operation; and there would be
equal debt service payments over the term of the bond issues. This would mean
that the state would have to make interest payments for two years before the
ferry commences operation; however, we assume that on average it could invest
half of the funds at 3 per cent interest. We also provide for financing and
other expenses along the line suggested by Eastman Dillon, Union Securities & Co.
This arrangement provides for equal debt service charges for 28 years.

We recognize that there are many other financial arrangements, far more
than we can mention here. For example, revenue bonds as well as general

obligation bonds could be issued in installments, as funds are required for capital expenditures. However, we did not receive any definite information on the timing of fund requirements. Another possibility mentioned by Eastman Dillon, Union Securities & Co. is to start amortization of the bond principal several years after the commencement of the ferry system, for example, the sixth year of operation, and to have increasing debt service charges over the life of the bonds. The advantage of this procedure is that debt service payments would be low during the early years of the operation and increase presumably as revenue grows larger. Yet for purposes of our estimates we consider equal debt service charges more appropriate as they tend to reflect the costs involved. Even so, they do not fully reflect the sharp depreciation of the ships during the early years of operation.

In Table IV-4 we also show the higher estimates of a possible revenue bond issue and annual debt service charges. In summary, the higher estimate is based upon higher costs for ships and terminal facilities, state expenditures for necessary harbor construction, revenue bonds for 30 years at 5 per cent interest, and amortization of bond principal over 28 years. Based on these conditions, the total bond issue amounts to $21,506,000, and the annual debt service is $1,443,000. On the other hand, in the lower estimate the total bond issue amounts to $14,052,000, and the annual debt service is $900,000. The lower cost estimate is based upon lower cost of ships, minimum terminal facilities, federal expenditures for all necessary harbor construction, general obligation bonds for 25 years at 3.5 per cent, and amortization of bond principal over 23 years.

Operating and administrative expenses.--The costs of operations comprise wages of crew including fringe benefits, crew subsistence, ship stores and

supplies, fuel oil, repair and maintenance of ships, insurance, and maintenance and operation of terminals.

In making our cost estimates we have used those in the Law and Wilson-Tudor report for fiscal year 1965 as a base. However, we have examined each major cost item and have adjusted each to calendar year 1965 with revisions to the extent we deemed advisable. In general, we have made two cost estimates, a lower and a higher one for calendar year 1965, and then we have projected each item to calendar year 1969, using annual increase cost factors. We should emphasize again that our lower and higher cost estimates are not minimum and maximum estimates, but rather a range of lower and higher cost estimates based upon different assumptions. We now discuss each major cost item.

The Law and Wilson-Tudor estimates of crew wages were based upon a minimum crew of 24 and three rotating shifts handling two ships. It was assumed that commissary facilities would be handled by a concessionaire under contract; he would provide all commissary personnel. We checked minimum crew requirements for purposes of safety with Coast Guard officials. On the basis of the type of ship, schedule and ferry service envisaged, the Coast Guard officials in charge of Honolulu Marine Inspection stated the following about crew requirements.[9] A minimum complement of 32 men who qualify as certificated lifeboatmen would be required under Coast Guard safety regulations. The following number of officers and crew would be required in this total:

1 - Master	6 - Able Seamen	1 - Chief Engineer
1 - Chief Mate	3 - Ordinary Seamen	1 - 1st Asst. Engineer
1 - 2nd Mate	3 - Radio Officers	1 - 2nd Asst. Engineer
1 - 3rd Mate	1 - Patrolman	1 - 3rd Asst. Engineer
		6 - Oilers

[9]Summarized from a letter from Commander John W. Yager, U.S. Coast Guard, Officer in Charge (Acting), Honolulu Marine Inspection, dated March 2, 1965.

109

However, if the hours of duty do not exceed 16 hours in any one day, the following
need not be carried:

1 - 3rd Mate	1 - Ordinary Seaman	1 - 3rd Asst. Engineer
2 - Able Seamen	1 - Radio Officer	2 - Oilers

Nevertheless, a minimum of 32 certificated lifeboatmen would be required on board
at all times. The safety requirements of the Coast Guard could be satisfied with
the minimum crew specified in the Law and Wilson-Tudor report if the concessionaire
provides at least nine men who can qualify as seamen to man lifeboats as well as
perform commissary duties. We recognize that this could present some problems,
but we understand that it is possible to find such workers. The Coast Guard
also indicated that each ship would have to have a qualified pilot familiar with
each of the harbors served. This could mean that more than one pilot might be
required at least for certain ports. Also, the Federal Communications Commission
might require additional radiomen for the trip between Honolulu and Nawiliwili
on Kauai.

Another important aspect would be the crew requirements and wages negotiated
with the unions involved. We did talk with some union leaders, but we did not
receive nor could we expect to receive any specific commitments from them.

We did examine copies of agreements negotiated by unions with the Alaska
Ferry System and also copies of agreements in effect for maritime activities in
this area. Analysis of these agreements and prevailing labor costs indicate
that the Law and Wilson-Tudor estimates of crew wages and other benefits for
1965 seem to be quite low in terms of the minimum crews, the shifts and schedules
specified, and the wage rates. We note that the union agreements for the Alaska
Ferry System provide for two crews per ship and 12 hour working days, six hours
on duty and six hours off duty. However, the pattern of the union agreements
for the Alaska Ferry System may not be especially relevant for Hawaii since the

110

Alaska Southeastern Ferry has longer voyages, including overnight trips. We also note that in the Alaska agreements the unions accepted the minimum crew requirements specified by the Coast Guard in the Certificate of Inspection.

As our lower estimate of crew wages and other benefits, we accept the minimum crew of 27 men specified by the Coast Guard for a trip of over 16 hours. In addition, we add a purser and nurse. This makes a total of 29 people. We assume that a concessionaire can provide at least four men, who can qualify as certificated lifeboatmen, so that the ship will carry the minimum required by the Coast Guard. Under the schedules used in the Law and Wilson-Tudor study, trips would be completed within 16 hours. It is realistic to plan for practically daily service to the major islands within 16 hours. Yet, in the case of trips to Hilo and in case of a short delay in disembarking and embarking passengers and handling automobiles and cargo at principal ports, the trips could readily exceed 16 hours per day. For that reason after consulting various maritime people, we are providing for a crew specified by the Coast Guard for a trip somewhat in excess of 16 hours per day. We assume that seamen will perform necessary cleaning in order to keep the ships clean for the comfort of passengers en route. Under this arrangement, a concessionaire would provide minimum personnel, including four men who would qualify as certificated lifeboatmen. Much of the food could be pre-cooked and prepared before departure of the ships; it could be served cafeteria or buffet style. Restaurant service could be supplemented by various vending machines. The estimate of crew wages provides little for overtime. In order to take care of more overtime, additional pilots, men to clean ships thoroughly while they are staying overnight after a trip, and other possible requirements, we are providing a contingency of 20 per cent.

111

The higher crew wages are based upon a complement of 32 officers and seamen. This includes the 27 officers and crew specified by the Coast Guard and a purser as in our lower estimate. In addition there would be four additional seamen, especially to keep the ship immaculate en route. Moreover, there would also be a nurse, a matron, and a hostess. This would be a total of 35 persons. The concessionaire would not be required to obtain personnel who could also qualify as certificated lifeboatmen. This might make a concession more attractive for a catering company. Onceagain we provide a 20 per cent contingency for additional overtime, extra pilots, extra cleaning personnel at ports while ships are docked overnight, and other possible requirements.

Both our lower and higher estimates of crew wages are based upon three crews rotating to operate two ships. They are also based upon 16 hour schedules of operation, but we recognize that some trips may slightly exceed 16 hours per day. Wage costs including benefits are projected to calendar year 1969 by using a compound growth factor of 4 per cent per year. This factor of 4 per cent was about the average of several estimates we received from companies and unions, based upon experience during the last five years.

Examining other crew costs, we find crew subsistence in the Law and Wilson-Tudor report to be low at $2.75 per day, based on a concessionaire providing food. The minimum amount we received from a caterer was $4.00 per man day; we use this amount in our low estimate. Our high cost estimate is based on a charge of $5.00 per man day by a concessionaire. Caterers gave this amount as a more realistic cost for feeding the men. For extra personnel and extra food on long trips we provide a contingency of 15 per cent.

The Law and Wilson-Tudor estimate of the costs of maintenance, repair and drydocking of each ship is based upon performing this work in Honolulu. However,

the only facilities which could handle drydocking of this size ship are those of the Navy at Pearl Harbor. The Navy usually only handles private ships in case of emergency. From checking with Navy officials in Honolulu we find that it is possible that special arrangements can be worked out with the Navy for drydocking the ferry ships at Pearl Harbor, as no private facilities are available. Approval would have to be obtained from Washington. Our lower estimate is based on drydocking in Honolulu. In this estimate we provide for two weeks loss of revenue which is considered as a cost. Drydocking would be undertaken presumably during a slack, off-season period when the loss of revenue would be at a minimum. Our higher estimate is based upon performing all possible maintenance and repair work in Honolulu and drydocking on the west coast. This would mean higher costs in taking the ships to the west coast and loss of revenue of about three weeks for each ship. Our cost estimate includes the possible loss of revenue for three weeks for each ship. Once again we presume that drydocking would be undertaken during a slack, off-season period to keep the loss of revenue at a minimum.

We have found the Law and Wilson-Tudor estimates of the cost of ship stores, equipment, fuel, and supplies to be reasonable. We, therefore, use them in our lower cost estimate. Our higher cost estimate of these items, except for insurance, is 10 per cent higher. Insurance underwriters stated that the estimate for insurance on ships is low and is based upon minimum coverage and some deductibles. Our higher estimate for insurance is obtained from an underwriter's estimate based on more complete coverage.

We consulted the chief and staff members of the Harbors Division on the anticipated costs of maintaining terminals, necessary personnel at terminals,

and anticipated administrative personnel and other expenses.[10] Staff members of the Harbors Division estimated the costs of maintaining each terminal at $15,000 to $20,000, which we use as our lower and higher estimates. They also stated that an agent, assistant agent, and a helper would be the minimum personnel required at each terminal, and they reviewed possible salaries. Finally, they reviewed administrative personnel, possible salaries under civil service, and other administrative expenses. In our lower estimate, we add another assistant agent and helper for Honolulu, and another assistant agent for both Maalaea and Kawaihae, and adjust salaries to prevailing levels. In our higher estimate we provide one additional man at each terminal to assist in expediting loading and unloading of passengers and cargo and performing various other duties. This makes a total of 22 workers in our lower estimate and 28 in our higher estimate to operate six terminals

Otherwise, in our lower cost estimate, we accept the Law and Wilson-Tudor report estimates for utilities and supplies at terminals, salaries of administrative personnel, with some adjustments of salaries to civil service scales, and other administrative expenses. Our low estimate also provides for minimum advertising estimated at $35,000 and has a contingency of 10 per cent for terminal and administrative expenses. Our higher cost estimate provides for additional administrative personnel that have been suggested by various maritime and business people. It also doubles advertising expenses and increases other terminal and office expenses. Finally, it provides 10 per cent contingencies for terminal and administrative expenses. The details on the major cost items for the lower and higher estimates are shown in Tables IV-5 and IV-6.

10Mr. Melvine E. Lepine, Chief, Harbors Division, Department of Transportation, and members of his staff were highly cooperative in going over possible costs.

114

TABLE IV-5

LOWER ESTIMATE OF ANNUAL OPERATING AND ADMINISTRATIVE
COSTS OF A FERRY SYSTEM, 1969
(Thousands of Dollars)

	Estimated Costs 1965		Annual Cost Increase Factor (Per Cent)	Estimated Costs 1969	
Operation of Each Ship					
Crew wages, including overtime, pensions, welfare, vacations, FICA	429		4.0	502	
Contingencies at 20 per cent	86			100	
		515			602
Crew subsistence estimated at $4.00 per man day	35		2.5	39	
Contingencies at 15 per cent	5			6	
		40			45
Ship stores, supplies and equipment		102	2.0		110
Other vessel expenditures		10	2.0		11
Fuel oil		213	1.5		226
Repair, drydocking and maintenance	75		4.0	88	
Contingencies at 20 per cent	15			18	
Loss of revenue	—	90		24	130
Insurance		197	2.0		213
Cost of Operating Each Ship		1,167			1,337
Cost of Operating Two Ships		2,334	2,334		2,674	2,674
Operation and Maintenance of Terminal Facilities					
Maintenance of 6 terminals at $15,000 per terminal		90	3.0		101
Personnel at terminals:			2.5		
6 agents at $6,000 each	36				
9 assistant agents at $5,000 each	45				
7 helpers and operating personnel at $4,000 each	28				
Wage benefits, including vacations, pensions, FICA	22				
		131			145
Utilities, supplies, rent, etc.		47	2.0		51
Contingencies at 10 per cent		27			30
Total Cost of Operating Terminals		295	295		327	327

115

TABLE IV-5--<u>Continued</u>

	Estimated Costs 1965	Annual Cost Increase Factor (Per Cent)	Estimated Costs 1969
<u>Administrative Expenses</u>			
Administrative personnel		2.5	
1 general manager	14		
1 assistant manager and operations chief	12		
1 accountant and purchasing agent	10		
1 superintendent engineer	10		
1 general passenger agent	8		
1 accounting clerk	5		
1 payroll clerk	5		
1 claims clerk	5		
1 executive secretary	5		
2 clerk typists	8		
Wage benefits, including vacations, pensions, FICA	<u>17</u>		
	99		109
Other office expenses	40	2.5	44
Advertising	35	2.5	39
Contingencies for administration at 10 per cent	<u>17</u>		<u>19</u>
Total Administrative Expenses	191 191		211 211
Total Annual Operation and Administrative Costs	2,820		3,212

116

TABLE IV-6

HIGHER ESTIMATE OF ANNUAL OPERATING AND ADMINISTRATIVE COSTS
OF A FERRY SYSTEM, 1969
(Thousands of Dollars)

	Estimated Costs 1965	Annual Cost Increase Factor (Per Cent)	Estimated Costs 1969	
Operation of Each Ship				
Crew wages, including overtime, pensions, welfare, vacations, FICA	497	4.0	581	
Contingencies at 20 per cent	99		116	
	596		697	
Crew subsistence estimated at $5.00 per man day	52	2.5	57	
Contingencies at 15 per cent	8		9	
	60		66	
Ship stores, supplies and equipment	112	2.0	121	
Other vessel expenditures	11	2.0	12	
Fuel oil	234	1.5	248	
Repair, drydocking and maintenance	95	4.0	111	
Contingencies at 20 per cent	19		22	
Loss of revenue	114		72	205
Insurance	247	2.0	267	
Cost of operating each ship	1,374		1,616	
Cost of operating two ships	2,748	2,748	3,232	3,232
Operation and Maintenance of Terminal Facilities				
Maintenance of 6 terminals at $20,000 per terminal	120	3.0	135	
Personnel at terminals:		2.5		
6 agents at $6,000 each	36			
9 assistant agents at $5,000 each	45			
13 helpers and operating personnel at $4,500	59			
Wage benefits, including vacations, pensions, FICA	28			
	168		185	
Utilities, supplies, rent, etc.	52	2.0	56	
Contingencies at 10 per cent	34		37	
Total Cost of Operating Terminals	374	374	413	413

117

TABLE IV-6--Continued

	Estimated Costs 1965	Annual Cost Increase Factor (Per Cent)	Estimated Costs 1969
Administrative Expenses			
Administrative personnel		2.5	
1 general manager	14		
1 assistant manager and operations chief	12		
1 sales and advertising executive	10		
1 comptroller and accountant	10		
1 purchasing agent	10		
1 superintendent engineer	10		
1 assistant engineer	9		
1 general passenger agent	8		
1 assistant passenger agent	7		
2 accounting clerks	12		
1 payroll clerk	5		
1 claims clerk	5		
3 secretaries	15		
4 clerk typists	16		
Wage benefits, including vacations, pensions, FICA	29		
	172		190
Other office expenses	65	2.5	72
Advertising	70	2.5	77
Contingencies for administration at 10 per cent	30		34
Total Administrative Expenses	337	337	373	373
Total Annual Operation and Administrative Costs		3,459	4,018

118

TABLE IV-7

LOWER AND HIGHER ESTIMATES OF TOTAL ANNUAL COSTS OF A FERRY SYSTEM
1969
(Thousands of Dollars)

	Lower Estimate	Mid-point Estimate	Higher Estimate
Debt service charges	900	1,172	1,443
Operation and maintenance of two ships	2,674	2,953	3,232
Operation and maintenance of terminals	327	370	413
Administrative expenses	211	292	373
Total Annual Costs	4,112	4,787	5,461

As we indicated before, we determined lower and higher estimates of operating ships, terminals, and administrative expenses for 1965. We then projected these costs to 1969 by using compound annual cost increase factors of 4 per cent for crew labor; 2.5 per cent for crew subsistence; 4 per cent for maintenance, repair and drydocking of ships; 2.5 per cent for administrative and terminal personnel, office expenses and advertising; 2 per cent for utilities, ships stores and various supplies; and 1.5 per cent for fuel. These annual cost increase factors were ascertained by consulting various maritime authorities on the experience of the last five years and consulting available cost indexes.

Table IV-5 shows the lower annual cost estimate for 1969, with a detailed breakdown for costs of operating ships and terminals and overall administration. The lower cost estimate for annual operating and administrative costs in 1969 amounts to $3,212,000. On the other hand, as Table IV-6 shows, the higher cost estimate for operating and administrative costs amounts to $4,018,000 in 1969. Once again we show detailed breakdowns of estimated costs of operating ships and terminals in the table.

In Table IV-7, we show the lower and higher total annual cost estimates of a ferry system in 1969, including the service charges. The lower total annual cost estimate in 1969 is $4,112,000; the higher annual cost estimate is $5,461,000. Table IV-7 also shows the mid-point cost estimate, which is $4,787,000. Once again we emphasize that the low and high estimates are neither minimum nor maximum estimates, but rather a range based upon different assumptions. With the detailed discussion and the tables shown in this chapter, it is possible to revise the cost estimates for a different set of assumptions.

120

3. Some Economic Aspects of Cost

Fixed and variable costs.--Economists usually distinguish between fixed

and variable costs in the short run. This distinction is often made in business

management with fixed costs referred to as overhead costs. Fixed costs are

those which do not vary with output in the short run such as administrative

expenses, interest on bonds, insurance, and a large portion of depreciation.

Variable costs, on the other hand, such as most labor, materials, fuel, and

supplies, tend to vary with output.

If it is assumed that there would be an unchanging daily operation of the

ferry between the major islands all year round, as defined in Chapter II, then

practically all costs may be considered as fixed, except possibly some maintenance

and minor wages. Thus, once a schedule is established and remains unchanged,

practically all costs become fixed regardless of the traffic handled by a ferry.

The costs would be the same whether the ferry is running completely full or

practically empty. On the other hand, if on the basis of experience the ferry

schedule is curtailed during the slack periods of the year, some of the costs,

especially fuel, ships stores, supplies, and possible wages, could be reduced

and would be semi-variable. Advertising costs, in turn, are discretionary, for

they can be increased or reduced by administrative decision. But they may be of

key importance in developing demand. It also should be considered that a

curtailment of schedule might have a seriously adverse impact on demand. Thus,

any effort to reduce costs has to carefully evaluate the ramifications on demand.

The distinction between fixed costs and variable costs is of some importance

from the standpoint of management of a ferry, as in many business enterprises.

When fixed or overhead costs, as they are frequently called in business, comprise

a substantial part of total costs, it is usually sound to price the product of

service to operate as close to full capacity as possible. This spreads the high fixed costs over a large volume. With respect to a ferry, for example, it might be advisable to have lower rates during the slack periods to encourage as many people as possible to use its service at those times.

A fixed charge of special importance in the operation of a ferry is debt service. Interest on the bonds involves a fixed charge to the state government that must be met until the bonds are repaid, even if the state ceases the ferry operation. Sale of bonds also involves amortization to provide funds for the repayment of bonds. From the standpoint of costs, the amortization may be considered to be the equivalent of depreciation charges. Depreciation depends upon the life of the ship and port facilities and is a fixed cost. It occurs irrespective of the extent of the use of the ferries. In fact, depreciation might increase if the ships are idle for considerable periods of time. Most of the administrative costs are also fixed and do not vary with changes in the schedules and frequency of ferry service, although possibly even some administrative costs might be reduced, if the service is curtailed.

Full measure of costs.--From the standpoint of economic analysis, the full costs of a ferry system probably are not reflected in the cost estimates we have made, as depreciation is not fully taken into account. Under level debt service charges, amortization of bond principal is relatively small during the early years and higher during the later years. On the other hand depreciation, especially of the ships and to some extent of the terminal facilities, would be large during the early years and would decline during the later years. Thus, amortization of bond principal is not the equivalent and is considerably less than the full depreciation during the early years or during the first half of the bond issue. Of course, if the ships and terminal facilities are used in

a ferry operation for a period of 25 to 30 years, then depreciation would be fully covered. Still from the economic standpoint that we have mentioned, costs are understated during the early years of operation.

Abandonment costs.--In many respects a more serious problem would be the cost involved to the state if a ferry system is not successful and the ships have to be disposed of. This would involve repayment of bonds outstanding and liquidation of the ferry system. Since amortization of bond principal does not reflect the decline in the value of ships, liquidation of a ferry system would involve serious losses or abandonment costs. The legislature as a decision-making body has to weigh the probability of success and the benefits involved against the risks and the losses involved in case of failure.

123

CHAPTER V

EXPECTED PROFIT AND LOSS STATEMENT FOR THE PROPOSED FERRY SYSTEM

Now that we have both the traffic estimates from Chapter III and cost estimates from Chapter IV, we are ready to answer the question: Would the proposed ferry pay for itself? First, we shall compute the average revenue per passenger round trip. Second, on the basis of previous traffic estimates, we shall find the expected total revenue for the first year of ferry operations. Third, we shall analyze these revenues and the estimated costs. Finally, we shall discuss the prospects for the ferry after its first year of operation.

1. Average Revenue Per Passenger Round Trip

State residents.--On the basis of the household survey, 58 per cent of the household trips for other than strictly business were made between Oahu and Kauai or Maui, 37 per cent between Oahu and Hawaii, and 5 per cent between Oahu and Molokai. It is reasonable to assume that the business round trips, representing about 9 per cent of all trips (Table III-1, column 1) were distributed the same way. Also, from the respondents who stated that their households would patronize the ferry system it was estimated that they represented a population of which about 66 per cent were 22 years old or older, 32 per cent between 2 and 21 years old, and 2 per cent under 2 years old. These percentages include business trips which, we assumed, involved adults only.

The above traffic and age percentages are shown under column 1 in Table V-1, where rows denoted by (a) include the percentage of adult ferry riders and (b) the percentage of travelers between 2 and 21 years old. Travelers under 2 years old will ride the ferries for free. Round trip fares shown in column 2 of this table represent fares for the proposed ferry system which are slightly higher than 50 per cent air fares (excluding tax). The product of each row shown

TABLE V-1

NET AVERAGE REVENUE PER PASSENGER ROUND TRIP
OF STATE RESIDENTS AT ABOUT 50 PER CENT AIR FARES

(Traffic and Age Percentages) (1)	X	(Round Trip Fare) (2)	=	(Fare per 100 Passengers) (3)
1. Honolulu - Kauai/Maui				
a) (0.58 x 0.66)	X	($13)	=	$ 497.64
b) (0.58 x 0.32)	X	(7)	=	129.92
2. Honolulu - Hawaii				
a) (0.37 x 0.66)	X	(20)	=	488.40
b) (0.37 x 0.32)	X	(10)	=	118.40
3. Honolulu - Molokai				
a) (0.05 x 0.66)	X	(7)	=	23.10
b) (0.05 x 0.32)	X	(4)	=	6.40
Sub-total revenue per 100 passengers				$1,263.86
4. Concessions				
$0.30 x 100			=	30.00
Gross revenue per 100 passengers				$1,293.86
Less: 5 per cent for discounts				64.70
Net revenue per 100 passengers				$1,229.16
Net average revenue per passenger round trip				$ 12.29

TABLE V-1

NET AVERAGE REVENUE PER PASSENGER ROUND TRIP
OF STATE RESIDENTS AT ABOUT 50 PER CENT AIR FARES

(Traffic and Age Percentages) (1)	X	(Round Trip Fare) (2)	=	(Fare per 100 Passengers) (3)
1. Honolulu - Kauai/Maui				
a) (0.58 x 0.58)	X	(213)	=	$ 697.64
b) (0.58 x 0.32)	X	(7)	=	129.92
2. Honolulu - Hawaii				
a) (0.37 x 2.66)	X	(20)	=	488.40
b) (0.37 x 0.52)	X	(10)	=	118.40
3. Honolulu - Molokai				
a) (0.05 x 0.66)	X	(7)	=	23.10
b) (0.05 x 0.22)	X	(6)	=	6.40
Sub-total revenue per 100 passengers				$1,263.86
4. Computation				
$0.50 x 100				50.00
Gross revenue per 100 passengers				$1,293.86
Less: 5 per cent for discounts				64.50
Net revenue per 100 passengers				$1,229.36
Net average revenue per passenger round trip				$ 12.29

in column 3 of Table V-1 is the revenue for 100 passengers for each combination of traffic and age percentages. To the total revenue of $1,263.86 per 100 passengers, $30 is added for concessions which according to Coverdale and Colpitts is "a typical revenue rate" for food, beverages, and other services rendered on board the ferries. Subtracting $64.70 for discounts, which represents 5 per cent of gross revenue, and dividing the net revenue by 100, we find that the net average revenue per passenger will be $12.29 under the above stated conditions.

Tourists.--We assume that about 88 per cent of the tourists who will patronize the ferry during the first year of operations will be 22 years old or older and 10 per cent between 2 and 21 years old. This assumption is in line with the available statistics. According to the statistics published by the Hawaii Visitors Bureau during 1962 and 1963 only 7.8 per cent of overnight visitors were less than 19 years old. Also, according to available statistics, 65 per cent of tourist visits were made either to Kauai or Maui while 35 per cent were made to the Big Island.

The above traffic and age percentages are shown in column 1 of Table V-2. Multiplying these percentages in each row by the corresponding round trip fare in column 2, we obtain the product in column 3 which represents the total revenue per 100 passenger round trips. Adding the amount from concessions and subtracting $73.50 for 5 per cent discounts, we obtain $13.97 as the net revenue per tourist round trip.

Automobiles.--For estimating total revenues from vehicular traffic we shall use an average flat rate of $20 for a round trip between any two islands. This rate is slightly less than the average rates of $35 and $8 used in the household survey and also less than half the present barge rate for a round trip within 15 days. It is also in line with the fact that the respondents in the household survey were not too sensitive to price rates for cars.

TABLE V-2

NET AVERAGE REVENUE PER TOURIST PASSENGER ROUND TRIP
AT ABOUT 50 PER CENT AIR FARE

(Traffic and Age Percentages) (1)	X	(Round Trip Fare) (2)	=	(Fare per 100 Passengers) (3)
1. Honolulu - Kauai/Maui				
a) (0.65 x 0.88)	X	($13)	=	$ 743.60
b) (0.65 x 0.10)	X	(7)	=	45.50
2. Honolulu - Hawaii				
a) (0.35 x 0.88)	X	(20)	=	616.00
b) (0.35 x 0.10)	X	(10)	=	35.00
Sub-total revenue per 100 passengers				$1,440.10
3. Concessions				
$0.30 x 100			=	30.00
Gross total revenue per 100 passengers				$1,470.10
Less: 5 per cent for discounts				73.50
Net revenue per 100 passengers				$1,396.60
Net average revenue per tourist round trip				$ 13.97

TABLE 9-2

NET AVERAGE TBA... PER TOURIST PASSENGER ROUND TRIP
AT ABOUT 50 PER CENT AIR FARE

Source of Patronage (Traffic and Age Percentages) (1)		Round Trip Fare (2)	Fare per 100 Passengers (3)
1. Honolulu - Kauai/Maui			
a) (0.65 x 0.88)	X	(513)	$ 742.80
b) (0.65 x 0.10)	X	(7)	45.50
2. Honolulu - Hawaii			
a) (0.55 x 0.88)	X	(20)	$ 616.00
b) (0.55 x 0.10)	X	(10)	35.00
Sub-total revenue per 100 passengers			$1,440.10
3. Concessions:			
$0.30 x 100			30.00
Gross total revenue per 100 passengers			$1,470.10
less: 5 per cent for discounts			73.50
Net revenue per 100 passengers			$1,398.60
Net average revenue per tourist round trip			$ 13.97

For commercial vehicles we shall use an average flat rate of $21 per commercial vehicle unit with three tons capacity per round trip between any two islands to be served by the proposed ferry system. This rate is equivalent to $7 per ton which is the average rate per ton of cargo transported by barge.

The reasons for the above rates for passenger cars and commercial vehicle units will be discussed in the next chapter which deals with the probable effects of the ferry system on the existing carriers.

Family rates.--No provisions have been made for family rates for the proposed ferry system. But the above passenger and car rates compare favorably with the existing air-barge family rates as shown in Table V-3. With full fare for the wife, family rates with the ferry represent slightly less than 50 per cent of regular family air fare-barge rates and about 55 per cent of family air fare-barge rates.

TABLE V-3

COMPARISON OF FAMILY RATES FOR A ROUND TRIP
WITH CAR BY AIR/BARGE AND FERRY

| Description | From Honolulu to: | |
	Kauai/Maui (1)	Hawaii (2)
1. Family of three		
a) Regular air fare-barge[1]	$108	$146
b) Family air fare-barge[1]	95	127
c) Ferry fare	53	70
2. Family of four		
a) Regular air fare-barge[1]	120	165
b) Family air fare-barge[1]	108	146
c) Ferry fare	60	80

[1] Barge rates for an automobile making a round trip within 15 days.

2. First Year of Operations: Profit or Loss?

Total revenue estimates.--The above average fare rates were used for estimating the total revenue (Table V-4) which the ferry system may realize during the first year of operations.

TABLE V-4

TOTAL REVENUE ESTIMATES OF THE PROPOSED FERRY SYSTEM
FIRST YEAR OF OPERATIONS
(Revenue Rounded to Thousands of Dollars)

Type of Traffic by Source	Lower (1)	Mid-point (2)	Upper (3)
1. Passenger			
a) State residents[1]/	$2,200	$2,675	$3,149
b) Tourists[2]/	791	869	947
Sub-total	$2,991	$3,544	$4,096
2. Automobiles			
a) State residents[3]/	$ 690	$ 842	$ 993
b) Tourists[3]/	57	62	68
c) Commercial[4]/	261	319	376
Sub-total	$1,008	$1,223	$1,437
Total	$3,999	$4,766	$5,533

[1]/Passenger traffic of state residents from Table III-6 multiplied by $12.29 (the net average revenue per round trip from Table V-1).

[2]/Tourist passenger traffic from Table III-6 multiplied by $13.97 (the net average revenue per round trip from Table V-2).

[3]/At $20 per car (traffic from Table III-6).

[4]/At $21 per commercial vehicle unit (traffic from Table III-6).

Note: Figures may not add up due to rounding.

2. First Year of Operation: Profit or Loss.

Total revenue estimates.--The above average fare rates were used for

estimating the total revenue (Table V-A) which the ferry system may realize

during the first year of operations.

TABLE V-A

TOTAL REVENUE ESTIMATES FOR THE PROPOSED FERRY SYSTEM
FIRST YEAR OF OPERATIONS
(Revenue rounded to thousands of dollars)

Type of Traffic by Source	Lower (1)	Mid-point (2)	Upper (3)
1. Passenger			
a) State residents[1]	52,202	52,673	57,143
b) Tourists[2]	795	862	937
Sub-total	52,997	53,534	58,096
2. Automobiles			
a) State residents	$ 650	$ 842	$ 994
b) Tourists[3]	67	87	68
c) Commercial[4]	281	319	376
Sub-total	57,005	57,223	57,637
Total	53,995	54,796	55,953

[1] Passenger traffic of state residents from Table III-D multiplied
by $12.29 (the net average revenue per round trip from Table V-4).

[2] Tourist passenger traffic from Table III-D multiplied by $16.50
(the net average revenue per round trip from Table V-2).

[3] At $4.920 per car (traffic from Table III-D). (V-2).

[4] At $21 per commercial vehicle (traffic from Table III-D).

Note. Figures may not add up due to rounding. (Table from item III-D).

129

In connection with the above total revenue estimates a number of points are important:

a. For reasons to be explained later we have used the conservative estimates for passenger traffic of state residents and for commercial traffic. Also, we have used the response to the roll-on, roll-off rather than the "piggyback" method of handling cargo.

b. In estimating the total revenue for the proposed ferry we used fares which are modal, based on the findings of our two surveys. Such fares are also consistent with the principle of complementarism of service between carriers which we shall explain in the next chapter. They may be used as guides to a diversified and more realistic structure of actual fares. Under the proposed scheduling and carrying capacity of the ferries, even the lower limit of the conservative traffic estimates of 235,610 passenger round trips and 49,792 vehicle round trips represents about 65 per cent for passengers and 68 per cent for vehicles of theoretical capacity. But traffic is likely to be quite seasonal. On the basis of the household survey, during the year prior to the interview as much as 49 per cent of pleasure household trips were made during the three summer months of June, July, and August. This experience is likely to be repeated with the ferry system, if and when established. Furthermore, traffic is likely to be concentrated on weekends and holidays. Such traffic patterns may require fares higher than the modal fares on weekends, holidays, and during the peak summer months, and lower than the modal fares on weekdays and the off-season months. Furthermore, it may be desirable to exclude commercial traffic on weekends and holidays.

Costs and revenues.--The expected annual operating expenses and revenues for the proposed ferry system during its first year of operations are shown in Table V-5. With this table we have reached a crucial point in our analysis.

130

TABLE V-5

EXPECTED OPERATING EXPENSES AND REVENUES
FOR THE PROPOSED FERRY SYSTEM
FIRST YEARS OF OPERATION
(Thousands of Dollars)

Operating	Upper-Lower (1)	Mid-point (2)	Lower-Upper (3)
1. Expenses[1]	$5,461	$4,787	$4,112
2. Revenues[2]	3,999	4,766	5,533
Profit (Loss)	($1,462)	($ 21)	$1,421

[1] From Table IV-7.

[2] From Table V-4.

We would like to focus the reader's attention on a number of considerations which are important if the figures in Table V-5 are used for the decision to approve or disapprove the proposed ferry system.

a. Interpretation of the figures in Table V-5 must be made in the light of the numerous assumptions and conditions stated in Chapters III and IV.

b. The cost and revenue estimates shown in Table V-5 were made by two researchers working independently of each other. This arrangement safeguarded us from unduly influencing each other's thinking in arriving at these estimates.

c. The decision to approve the ferry involves two major outlays: (a) the initial investment for building the two ferries and for constructing the required terminals, (b) the probable deficit involved in operating the ferry system. In cases such as this where a decision involves large sums of money, a decision maker would like to know the worst consequences of a wrong decision. For this reason we based our analysis on the conservative projected traffic revenue estimates. Also, for the same reason, in Table V-5 the upper cost estimated figure is placed against the lower projected traffic revenue estimate.

d. Conversion of the projected estimates of physical traffic to traffic revenue was done on the basis of ferry rates, representing about 50 per cent of air-barge rates which we consider modal.

e. In Chapter III we stated that in following the conservative viewpoint we would assign subjective probabilities to the projected traffic estimates obtained from the household and cargo surveys. Although estimates of tourist traffic were not obtained from a probability sample survey, we can also assign such subjective probabilities to these estimates. After careful evaluation of the variables involved (especially the fact that traffic estimates in Table III-6 represent aggregates without consideration of seasonal factors, and that conversion of physical traffic to traffic revenue involves another important variable, namely price), we would like to interpret the figures in Table V-5 as follows: (a) there is about a 40 per cent chance that the ferry system may break even during the first year of operations; (b) there is about a 5 per cent chance that the ferry operations may result in a surplus of about $1,421,000; and (c) there is about 10 per cent chance that a deficit from the ferry system may exceed $1,46^2,000 during the first year of operations.

The first year of ferry operations will be a very crucial one. Every effort must be made for an efficient operation with respect to such matters as scheduling orderly embarkation and disembarkation of passengers and vehicles, punctuality in departures and arrivals, and good service on board the vessels-- matters which are very important for securing wide acceptance of the ferry system by the public. In this connection, a number of suggestions may be helpful for implementing a decision to establish the ferry system, if such a decision is made.

a. The household and cargo surveys indicate that there is a fairly strong unfavorable image of surface transportation with respect to comfort at sea. Whether such an attitude is the result of past, actual experience is not material.

132

What matters is that erasing such an image, to the extent that it exists, and building public acceptance may require more than reliance on the advanced design of the ferries which promises a smooth ride. Thus, during at least the first six months, if not the first full year, of operations the ferry may serve the ports located on the leeward side of the islands only. Such a routing would minimize the likelihood of an adverse experience for persons who may look for evidence to justify their apprehensions; allow for the most favorable scheduling, permitting strict adherence to timing; and minimize the unfavorable impact of unforseen operational problems.

b. During this "trial" period, it may be even desirable to consider limiting the use of the ferries to passenger car traffic only. Although such a measure may curtail revenues somewhat, it may secure better passenger service and facilitate handling of unforseen operational problems. At the end of the "trial" period the ferry system may be open to commercial vehicular traffic on the basis of established patterns of passenger car traffic.

c. Also, during this "trial" period an intensive and systematic survey may be made for the purpose of collecting information from the users of the ferry system which may help to improve its operation. The experience gained from the "trial" period and the information from the survey will be helpful for deciding whether service should be extended to the ports on the windward side.

d. Before the ferry system begins to operate and during the "trial" period an intensive advertising campaign should be carried out. Unlike regular advertising, which will be designed to increase the traffic for the ferry system, this intensive campaign should have as its primary objective the elimination of any preconceived ideas which the public may have about surface passenger transportation between the islands. For the success of such a campaign it will be necessary to secure the close cooperation of all communication media in the state.

e.. The above recommendations are designed to influence favorably the revenue side of ferry operations. But the cost side should not be neglected In fact, we believe that there are more opportunities for exerting a greater control on costs than on revenues; and the state administration should make a special effort to keep down construction, as well as administrative costs.

3. Future Prospects

The above analysis dealt with expectations in the short run; at this point it is pertinent to raise the question: What are the cost and revenue prospects for the ferry system after the first year of operation?

Technical limitations.--We have already seen that there are a number of limitations which reduce the degree of reliability we can possibly have on our projected first-year estimates. These limitations become much more severe for later-year estimates since there are a number of distinctively assignable causes which greatly reduce the degree of reliability on projections of time series, i.e., numerical cost and revenue estimates on a year-to-year basis.

a . On the cost side, the most important item in the long run may prove to be operational costs, labor costs in particular. On the basis of experience in similar situations and the existing labor conditions in the State of Hawaii we are inclined to think that labor costs are likely to increase. But by how much and how fast we are unable to assess.

b . Our surveys have clearly shown that a considerable degree of doubt exists in the minds of a large segment of the population about comfort at sea. It is true that naval architects have assured us that modern ships especially designed to travel in rough waters can secure maximum comfort. Also, there is the experience of the ferry operating between Melbourne and Devonport in Tasmania, Australia, which evidently operates successfully in waters as rough as the waters

found in the channels between the Hawaiian Islands. Nevertheless, on the basis of the evidence we have obtained from our surveys, comfort at sea must be a second assignable cause whose probable outcome we are in no position to assess.

c. Last but not least is the possibility that, after public acceptance is secured, the ferry system may prove to be a startling success.

On technical grounds, therefore, the available evidence does not offer sufficient empirical foundations to justify time series projections. On the other hand, we have sufficient information which permits us to analyze the probable effects of the ferry system in terms other than projections of time series. This will be done in Part III of our report.

Prospects for rapid growth of traffic.--In the meantime, in concluding this chapter, we may examine the following question: Assuming that the first year experience proves partially satisfactory with a deficit, what are the prospects for traffic revenues closing the deficit gap?

After the ferry system receives initial acceptance by the public, a number of factors exist which strongly suggest that ferry traffic may grow quite rapidly.

In the first place, there are reasons to believe that latent sources of traffic for the ferry may exist among state residents.

a. We have already explained that the response we received from the household survey is very likely to under-report intentions of state residents to use the ferry system, by at least 10 per cent above the traffic volume used for our analysis shown in Table V-5.

b. But greater under-reporting than the above seems to be associated with the number of people per household round trip. This is so because the intention to travel on the ferry was associated with the previous experience of traveling by air which, on the average, involved two persons per household round trip. In view of the fact that there are about four persons per household, it is evident that the responses we received from the household survey underestimate the potential ferry traffic considerably.

c. Approximately 40 per cent of the ferry travel by state residents represents a net addition to inter-island travel. In view of the previous arguments we believe this new traffic is underestimated. This belief is further substantiated by the fact that stay-at-home vacations are widely practiced among the island residents, which might have been an important reason for inhibiting a more favorable response of intentions to travel on the ferry. Thus, the ferry system may prove to be an effective factor for undermining this habit of vacationing at home; it may generate additional new traffic.

d. The availability of vacation sites may prove to be a strong traffic generating factor. When respondents were questioned about the likelihood of taking at least one vacation at one of these vacation facilities during the 12 months subsequent to the interview (if the resorts were operating), respondent replies resulted in an estimate of approximately 35,000 households which would take such vacations. This estimate represents about 23 per cent of the 153,000 households represented by the household study. This response was based on the assumption that a ferry service would not be available. However, when respondents were questioned regarding the likelihood that the proposed vacation sites would be used if the ferry was available, their replies resulted in an estimate of about 65,000 households, or about 43 per cent of all represented households, which expect to use the resort facilities at least once during the 12-month period following the interview. These figures represent averages of the estimates based on the actual responses at 70 per cent and 30 per cent air fares.

e. Research findings from other studies show a close direct association between a growing propensity for travel- vacations and rising personal income. Such an association was also found in our household survey. Rising personal incomes, therefore, may be considered as another important factor for a traffic volume higher than the one recorded in the household survey by the time the ferry system is in operation.

f. Finally, another potential source of traffic may be tapped with the establishment of special group rates for business, civic, and other organizations.

In the second place, the ferry may attract tourist traffic as large or larger than the potential traffic from the state residents. Although no survey was conducted of tourist traffic, the limited information we have available points to the possibility that the ferry may prove to be one of the best tourist attractions in the Hawaiian Islands.

a. The newly established ferry system in Alaska has been a strong tourist attraction since it offers an opportunity for the tourist to admire the magnificent coastline of Southern Alaska. Similarly, the proposed ferry system in Hawaii may prove to be a strong tourist attraction by offering an opportunity to admire the scenic semi-tropical coastal line of the islands.

b. A large number of tourists visit the Hawaiian Islands in organized tours or package arrangements which provide for numerous sightseeing tours in the islands. We cannot imagine that even a single travel agency on the mainland would refuse to recognize that a ride on the proposed ferry is a tourist attraction equal to or better than many it has presently available.

After initial acceptance of the ferry system by the public, the extent to which ferry traffic will be sustained and grow may depend on a number of measures.

a. We have already pointed out that the proposed inter-island sea ferry should be looked upon as a system. The results of the household survey point out conclusively that the proposed vacation-recreation facilities must be considered as an integral part of this system. Most of them, if not all, must be available by the time the ferry is ready to operate.

b. Our personal tours of the neighboring islands, however, point out the need for further expanding the scope of the proposed ferry system. If the sea ferry is envisaged as a "sea highway" offering a mass transportation facility for

passengers and cars, the road network of the neighboring islands must be considered as an integral part of the ferry system. This road network in the neighbor islands must be improved considerably. Otherwise, the initial trip of Oahu residents to the outer islands may be rather discouraging. Since the bulk of resident traffic would originate from Oahu, lack of an improved network of roads in the neighbor islands may create a serious problem for sustaining desirable traffic flows for an economically self-supporting ferry system.

c.. Furthermore, to maintain the ferry traffic at desirable levels it may be necessary to consider natural "wonders" such as waterfalls, canyons, and volcanos as part of the proposed ferry system. To the out-of-state tourist these natural sights may be of secondary importance to the sandy beaches and the climate; but to the state residents such natural sights are likely to be the primary points of attraction since he can enjoy in general the same climate and comparable beaches in his home island. A few sights such as Iao Valley on Maui and the volcano area on Hawaii are well developed. But access to other sights such as the road to Waimea Canyon on Kauai, the road from Kahului to the waterfalls in Hana, and the road to Haleakala Crater on Maui require considerable improvement. In some other cases such as the road leading to the lookout at Wailua waterfalls on Kauai, improvement is badly needed. Also, a system announcing visibility condition in Waimea Canyon on Kauai and Haleakala volcano on Maui is highly desirable. It may go a long way in reducing the great disappointment that tourists experience from spending half a day and being unable to enjoy the view because they were not informed of poor weather conditions.

d. Finally, after initial public acceptance of the ferry, a sustained advertising campaign may be desirable or even necessary. Such a campaign may concentrate on an attempt to change the widespread habit of stay-at-home vacations. Also, if travel agencies and national communication media are well informed about

the availability of the ferry system, such a system may receive free publicity worth thousands of dollars.

Through measures such as the above, with careful planning, efficient adminis-tration, and the incorporation of suggestions such as those made in Chapters IV and V, on controlling costs and influencing traffic revenue, the ferry system--if established--may go a long way toward securing an operation free of deficit financing.

PART III

THE PROPOSED FERRY AS A PUBLIC UTILITY
AND ITS EXPECTED IMPACT ON THE ECONOMY

In Part II we examined the proposed ferry system as a private concern. Our analysis was focused on whether the ferry is likely to be a financially self-supporting undertaking. In this part of our report we analyze the available information, within the limits imposed by time and resources, in order to evaluate the effect which the proposed ferry system may have on the state economy. In Chapter VI we examine the probable effect which the proposed ferry may have on existing carriers. The probable effect of the proposed ferry on the state economy is discussed in Chapter VII. The proposed ferry as a factor for stimulating the economy of the neighbor islands is the subject matter of Chapter VIII. Finally, in Chapter IX we present an economic model to show from the analytical standpoint the probable long-run effects of the proposed ferry on the economy of Hawaii.

CHAPTER VI

THE FERRY AS A "FREE" HIGHWAY
ITS PROBABLE EFFECT ON EXISTING CARRIERS

In Chapter II we specified that the primary purpose of the proposed ferry would be to supply a transportation facility for the mass movement of people and cars between the major islands of Hawaii. In this respect, the proposed ferry may be considered as an alternative to a highway or as a "highway of the seas." We shall examine this proposition as an introduction to the whole analysis of Part III of our report and to the subject matter of the present chapter.

1. The Ferry as a "Free" Highway

From the viewpoint of construction and operational costs the proposed ferry may be considered as a "toll" road. In this respect, the ferry is comparable to a privately run concern, where the expected revenue must be sufficient to amortize the initial investment of the road and cover its operational costs. But a transportation facility such as the proposed one by the nature of its operations may be considered as a free highway rendering services to the public like any other highway in the state. If we accept this concept, then it might be worth our while to compare the ferry with a hypothetical highway linking the major Hawaiian islands.

A hypothetical highway.--We made a request to the Department of Transportation of the State of Hawaii for cost estimates of a two-lane and a four-lane hypothetical highway linking the major islands of Kauai, Oahu, Molokai, Maui, and Hawaii. These costs estimates are shown in Table VI-1.

In evaluating the above cost estimates the reader should keep in mind the following qualifications.

TABLE VI-1

TOTAL COST ESTIMATES OF A HYPOTHETICAL TWO- AND FOUR-LANE HIGHWAY LINKING THE MAJOR HAWAIIAN ISLANDS

Channel	Distance (Miles)	Total Costs	
		Two-Lane ($000)	Four-Lane ($000)
Kauai-Oahu	71.5	$18,018	$35,750
Oahu-Molokai	21.0	5,292	10,500
Molokai-Maui	10.0	2,520	5,000
Maui-Hawaii	23.5	5,922	11,750
Total	126.0	$31,752	$63,000

Source: Department of Transportation, State of Hawaii.

a. The cost estimates for construction and for rights-of-way are based on two projects, each involving a two-lane highway, one in the Kau area and the other in the Kawaihae area on the Big Island. Preliminary engineering and construction engineering costs were based on past highway projects in the state.

b. The unit cost for a two-lane highway is $252,000 per mile and for a four-lane highway $500,000 per mile. The unit cost for a two-lane highway is slightly more than half the unit cost for a four-lane highway because of safety factors, the cost of requiring room for passing, and extra space for emergencies.

c. These unit cost estimates represent minimum costs for building highways in the State of Hawaii. They involve no expensive curves and exclude interchanges. Also, they involve dry, flat, and inexpensive land, and include minimum requirements for drainage with no bridges or structures of large magnitude. For the sake of comparison the maximum unit cost of a four-lane highway H-2 with similar specifications is $1,920,000 per mile.

-142-

d. The mileage shown in Table VI-1 does not represent the shortest distance between two islands, but distances between points of connections to existing roads or highways for easy access to each island.

e. According to the State Department of Transportation for the fiscal year 1962-63 the statewide average maintenance cost per mile for both a two-lane or a four-lane highway was $4,500 and the minimum $2,000. On those bases, the annual average total maintenance cost for our hypothetical highway will be $567,000 and the minimum $252,000.

The alternative cost concept.--How do the construction and maintenance costs of the hypothetical highway compare with such estimated costs for the proposed ferry?

a. Such a hypothetical highway would most likely be eligible for federal aid participation on a 50-50 basis in view of the fact that it would connect the principal cities and towns of the state, but not on a 90-10 basis since the state's quota of this type of federal aid has been already used up. Assuming such 50 per cent federal aid is secured, the cost to the state will be $15,876,000 for a two-lane and $31,500,000 for a four-lane highway. Thus, the construction cost for the two ships and for the terminals of the proposed ferry system, which according to our estimates may range between $13,472,000 and $19,289,000 with a mid-point at $16,381,000, compares favorably with the construction costs of the least expensive hypothetical two-lane highway. On the other hand, it must be remembered that the above costs of the proposed ferry do not include the cost of developing the proposed vacation sites. We assumed that such vacation sites will be available at the time the ferry is in operation. On that assumption, we included the extra traffic of 9,000 household round trips which, according to our household survey, these sites may generate although the cost of such vacation sites will be covered by general state and federal funds, i.e., taxes.

b.   However, the annual maintenance costs for the proposed ferry system, i.e., ships and terminals which, according to our estimates, may range between $371,000 and $559,000 with a mid-point at $465,000, compares favorably with the average maintenance cost of $567,000 of our hypothetical highway.

Of course, no one argues that such a hypothetical highway is possible. The above cost comparisons were made by applying the alternative cost idea. For if such a hypothetical highway were possible and desirable, then the decision to approve the proposed ferry would have to be made by taking into consideration the costs involved in the alternative facility, namely a highway. A situation of this kind occurred in the State of Alaska. Although from the engineering standpoint most of the natural obstacles for a highway linking the major communities of Southern Alaska could have been surmounted, the construction and maintenance costs were so high that from the financial standpoint a ferry system was decidedly preferable.

A "free" highway of the seas.--Furthermore, conceiving the proposed ferry as a "free" highway of the seas raises the argument as to whether the construction and maintenance costs, like similar costs of a free highway, should be covered by general state funds. Assuming that such an argument is valid, the profit and loss statement of the proposed ferry system may look like the one shown on Table VI-2.

It is interesting to note that the Alaska ferry system is established as a free highway operating on an appropriation from the state general fund. Of course, there is a great difference between the case of the Alaska ferry system and the proposed ferry system in Hawaii with respect to physical, economic and social conditions. We brought up the alternative cost and the free highway concepts because we feel that in making an important decision such as this, these concepts

144

TABLE VI-2

EXPECTED OPERATING EXPENSES AND REVENUES FOR THE PROPOSED FERRY SYSTEM
IF CONSIDERED AS A "FREE" HIGHWAY, FIRST YEAR OF OPERATIONS
(Thousands of Dollars)

Operating	Upper-Lower (1)	Mid-point (2)	Lower-Upper (3)
1. Total operating expenses	$5,461	$4,787	$4,112
2. Minus amortization-maintenance[1]	2,002	1,637	1,271
3. Adjusted operating expenses	$3,459	$3,150	$2,841
4. Operating revenues	3,999	4,766	5,533
Surplus: rows 4 - 3	$ 540	$1,616	$2,692

[1] Includes interest charges. Tables IV-5 and IV-6 and IV-7.

should be taken into consideration, together with the scores of points already mentioned as well as other points which will be discussed in this and the remaining chapters of our report.

2. Probable Effect of the Ferry on Existing Airlines

One important primary interest group which is likely to be affected by the establishment of the proposed ferry system is represented by the airlines engaged in intra-Hawaii air services. First, we shall make projected estimates of the airline revenues which are likely to be diverted to the proposed ferry in 1969, the first year of ferry operations. Second, we shall express these projected estimates as per cent of projected airline passenger and total operating revenues. Third, we shall discuss prospects after the first year of ferry operations.

Estimates of revenue diversion.--In Chapter III we pointed out that on the basis of the household survey results, 15,000 business and 38,000 household round trips were estimated as the traffic which is likely to switch from the airlines

to the proposed ferry system. After multiplying the above number of household trips by 2.085, the average number of persons per household trip reported by the survey, and adding the above business trips, we arrive at a total point estimate of about 94,000 passenger round trips for 1965. The lower and upper estimates are 77,100 and 110,920 passenger round trips, respectively. These estimates were projected to 1969 by a factor of 1.17, representing a 4 per cent compound growth factor as was shown in projecting the total demand for the ferry in Chapter III.

These projected estimates are shown in row 1 of Table VI-3.

TABLE VI-3

ESTIMATES OF AIRLINE REVENUE DIVERSION
TO THE PROPOSED FERRY
FIRST YEAR OF OPERATIONS

Item	Lower (1)	Mid-point (2)	Upper (3)
1. Diverted traffic of			
a) State residents[1]	90,207	109,980	129,776
b) Tourists[2]	28,300	31,090	33,880
c) Total	118,507	141,070	163,656
2. Diverted revenue			
a) Per passenger[3]	$ 27	$ 27	$ 27
b) Total ($000)[4]	3,200	3,809	4,419

[1] Based on the interval estimates of the household survey from Table III-1 where the lower, mid-point, and upper limits of diverted traffic were 77,100, 94,000, and 110,920 of passenger round trips, respectively, for 1965 projected to 1969 by a factor 1.17 representing a 4 per cent compound factor.

[2] Half of tourist passenger round trips shown in Table III-6.

[3] Average passenger revenue per round trip excluding subsidies.

[4] Obtained by multiplying rows 1c x 2a.

-146-

Furthermore, we added to these projected estimates half of the tourist passenger round trips shown in Table III-6. Thus, we obtained the total number of passenger round trips for the lower, mid-point, and upper figures shown in row 1c of Table VI-3, which represents the passenger air traffic likely to be diverted to the proposed ferry.

The diverted revenue per passenger represents twice the earned yield per passenger reported in 1964. It was obtained as follows: the reported 1,145,614 (Civil Aeronautics Board, Form 41) were adjusted to 1,127,000 in order to represent passenger single trips. Then the 1964 reported passenger revenue (excluding subsidies) of $15,215,947 was divided by the above figure to obtain $13.50, which represents airline earnings per passenger single trip for 1964. This figure compares closely with the $13.41 revenue per passenger reported for the fiscal year ending June 30, 1964. (Air Transport Association of America, Civil Aeronautics Board, Form 41.) Multiplying the $27 earnings per passenger round trip by the projected estimates of the diverted traffic, we obtain the total airline revenue shown in row 2b of Table VI-3, which is likely to be diverted to the proposed ferry during the first year of operations. According to our cargo survey no air cargo is likely to be diverted to the proposed ferry system.

In interpreting these revenue diversions the following should be kept in mind.

a. For reasons explained earlier no objective probabilities may be stated for the revenue figures reported in row 2b, Table VI-3.

b. The assumptions made in Chapter III for projecting over-all traffic for the proposed ferry hold true in the present case.

c. We assume that the $27 earnings per passenger round trip will remain about the same through 1969.

d. On the basis of the household survey the average number of persons per household who are likely to switch to the ferry is slightly larger than the number of persons per household likely to continue using the airlines. However, the effect of household on revenues is likely to be offset by the fact that the proportion of children in the switching households is slightly larger than the proportion of children in the non-switching households.

Airlines versus revenue diversion.--In order to see the relationship between the above projected estimates of revenue diversion and airline revenues we need to project the latter through 1969.

This was done as follows: The 1964 reported 1,145,614 originations were projected to 1,683,000 and 2,019,000 by applying an 8 per cent and a 12 per cent annual compound factor. These compound factors are less than the ones used for finding the conservative and liberal projections of tourist traffic for 1969 in Chapter III to account for slower growth in traffic of local residents. Then the 1964 reported $15,215,947 passenger airline revenue (excluding subsidies) and $17,898,023 total airline revenue were divided by the 1,145,614 originations to obtain $13.28 and $15.62 revenues per origination, respectively. Finally, these revenues per origination were multiplied by the projected 1,683,000 and 2,019,000 originations to obtain the passenger and total revenues for 1969, recorded in row 1b of Table VI-4. It is important to note that the mid-points of these projections are close to the projection which could be obtained by using the annual growth factor recommended by Aloha Airlines.

It must be remembered that these airline revenue projections are based on a number of conditions.

a. The assumptions made for projecting tourist traffic for the ferry in Chapter III are also assumed in the present case.

148

TABLE VI-4

ESTIMATED DIVERSION OF AIRLINE REVENUES AS PER CENT
OF PROJECTED PASSENGER AND TOTAL AIRLINE REVENUES
(Absolute Figures in Thousands of Dollars)

	Upper-Lower (1)	Mid-point (2)	Lower-Upper (3)
1. Passenger revenue only			
a) Passenger revenue diversions[1]	$ 4,419	$ 3,809	$ 3,200
b) Airline revenue[2]	22,350	24,568	26,786
c) Per cent of diversion[3]	19.8%	15.5%	12.0%
2. Total revenue			
a) Passenger revenue diversions[1]	$ 4,419	$ 3,809	$ 3,200
b) Airline revenues[2]	26,289	28,898	31,506
c) Per cent of diversion[3]	16.8%	13.2%	10.2%

[1] From Table VI-3.

[2] Based on $15,216,000 passenger operating revenues excluding subsidies and $17,898,000 total operating revenues including subsidies for 1964 projected to 1969.

[3] Rows a divided by b.

Source: Civil Aeronautics Board, Form 41 for 1964 originations and revenues.

b.   Also, we assume that revenue per origination will remain about the same through 1969.

The percentage of airline revenues which is likely to be diverted to the proposed ferry system for the lower, mid-point, and upper figures are shown in rows 1c and 2c of Table VI-4. In interpreting these percentages a number of points should be kept in mind.

a.   These estimated percentages of revenue diversion hold true under the assumption that no reduction of air fares will take place prior to or during the first year of ferry operations.

b. Consistent with the analysis of expected profit and loss statement of the proposed ferry system presented in Chapter V, the percentages of revenue diversion shown in Table VI-4 were obtained by placing the lower and upper airline revenues in juxtaposition to the upper and lower revenue diversion, respectively.

c. However, for an important decision such as the proposed ferry system, it might be advisable to rely on the upper-lower, 19.8 per cent and 16.8 per cent representing the worst of the consequences, rather than on the mid-point or lower-upper percentages.

Prospects after the first year of ferry operations.--The above analysis is static in the sense that it is based on the household survey results and projections and it does not take into consideration the forces which may be released by the introduction of the proposed ferry. For example, projective studies of the Alaska ferry system estimated that about 6.7 per cent of air traffic was likely to be diverted to the ferry. Uncomfirmed reports from airline managers indicate that instead of a reduction in air traffic the Alaska ferry did in fact generate additional air traffic.

Although air traffic volume in the territory served by the Alaska ferry represents a small fraction of the inter-island air traffic in Hawaii and the percentage of estimated diversion is far less than the mid-point estimates for Hawaii, we feel that the effect of the ferry system on air traffic may follow a similar course, at least in part, of the experience in Alaska for a number of reasons.

a. Assuming that no reduction of air fares takes place, some of the diverted air traffic may return to the airlines when the novelty of the ferry wears off.

b. Of course, the volume of regained traffic is likely to be larger if the Civil Aeronautics Board approves a reduction in fares. While such a reduction

will be a direct benefit to the users of airline carriers, the loss of airline revenues need not be a complete loss to the economy of the islands. It is likely to be covered in part by federal subsidies.

c. In Chapter V we mentioned a number of factors which are likely to stimulate traffic for the ferry. Factors such as the availability of vacation sites, special group rates, rising incomes, improvement of tourist attractions, better roads, and the stimulation of new economic activity which the ferry may bring about may generate additional air traffic which may at least partially offset the initial loss of air traffic.

d. If the ferry proves to be a tourist attraction, special arrangements, for example, may provide for a trip to an island on the ferry one way and a return trip by air. Arrangements such as these may generate additional traffic for the airlines.

In sum, the proposed ferry system may prove to be a valuable alternative mode of transporting passengers, supplementing the existing air transport facilities, especially during peak holiday and seasonal periods.

3. Probable Effect of the Ferry on the Existing Barge Line

Another important primary interest group which is likely to be affected by the establishment of the proposed ferry system is represented by the barge line First, we shall make projected estimates of the barge revenues which are likely to be diverted to the proposed ferry under the roll-on, roll-off method in 1969, the first year of ferry operations. Second, we shall express these projected estimates of revenue diversion as per cent of projected revenues of the barge line. Third, we shall discuss the "piggyback" method of cargo handling and long-run prospects. All data in this section was obtained from the records of the barge line and the cargo survey described in Chapter III.

151

Estimates of revenue diversion under the roll-on, roll-off method.--On the basis of the data obtained from the cargo survey we found in Chapter III that the 1969 projected estimates of cargo traffic for the ferry under the roll-on, roll-off method of handling cargo were as shown in row 1 of Table VI-5. Multiplying these tonnage diversions by $7, representing the average revenue per short ton carried by the barge line, we obtain the cargo revenue diversions, shown in row 2 of the table.

The above cargo revenue diversions do not include the loss of revenue from the traffic of passenger cars carried by the barge line. On the basis of the record supplied by the barge line, such traffic has grown at a compound rate of about 7.5 per cent annually since 1960. We estimate that during 1969 the barge line is likely to carry between 8,000 and 9,000 passenger cars, including new cars shipped by dealers. These figures represent a compound factor of about 5 per cent and 7 per cent, respectively. Assuming that all this car traffic is likely to switch to the ferry and multiplying these figures by $45, representing a conservative average freight revenue per car, we obtain the revenue of the barge line which is likely to be lost to the ferry from this type of traffic. The sum of the two revenue diversions is shown in the bottom row of Table VI-5.

TABLE VI-5

ESTIMATES OF BARGE REVENUE DIVERSION TO THE PROPOSED FERRY
UNDER THE ROLL-ON, ROLL-OFF METHOD, FIRST YEAR OF FERRY OPERATIONS

	Lower (1)	Mid-point (2)	Upper (3)
1. Cargo diversion (tons)[1]	37,329	45,522	53,715
2. Cargo revenue diversion[2]	$261,000	$319,000	$376,000
3. Automobile revenue diversion[3]	360,000	383,000	405,000
4. Total revenue diversion; rows 2 + 3	$621,000	$702,000	$781,000

[1] Multiplying row 2c of Table III-6, by 3 tons.
[2] Multiplying row 1 by $7.
[3] Multiplying estimated car traffic of 8,000, 8,500, and 9,000 for 1969 by $45.

152

The following points are important for interpreting the above estimated revenue diversions of the barge carrier.

a. Again, for reasons explained in Chapter III, no objective probabilities may be stated for these estimated revenue diversions.

b. All the assumptions made in Chapter III for projecting the cargo traffic for the proposed ferry are equally valid in the present case.

c. We assume that the freight revenue of $7 per short ton and $45 per car earned presently by the bargo carrier will remain about the same through 1969.

d. The above estimated revenue diversions for cargo are based on our cargo survey which covered the credit shippers of the existing barge line, only. Coverage of cash shippers, i.e., shippers who are rather irregular and do not carry a credit account with the company, required a separate survey which neither time nor resources permitted. Revenue from cash shippers represented 23 per cent in 1963 and 24 per cent in 1964 of total freight revenue. Although we cannot tell how much of this revenue is likely to be diverted to the proposed ferry, we feel that revenue diversion from this type of cargo is likely to be substantial in view of the fact that cash shippers are likely to represent persons shipping small quantities which can be easily carried on passenger cars, especially station wagons.

The barge line versus revenue diversion.--In order to express the above estimated revenue diversions in relation to the total revenue of the barge line, we need to project the carrier's revenues through 1969.

The required projections are shown in Table VI-6, row 2. They were obtained by applying to the 1964 revenue of $4,138,000 a 6 per cent compound factor for the lower projection of about $5,538,000 and an 8 per cent compound factor for the upper projection of about $6,081,000.

153

TABLE VI-6

ESTIMATED DIVERSION OF BARGE REVENUES
AS PER CENT OF PROJECTED BARGE REVENUES
(Absolute Figures Represent Thousands of Dollars)

	Upper-Lower (1)	Mid-point (2)	Lower-Upper (3)
1. Revenue diversion[1]	$ 781	$ 702	$ 621
2. Gross revenue estimates[2]	5,538	5,810	6,081
3. Per cent of revenue diversion; row 1 ÷ 2	14.1%	12.1%	10.2%

[1] Table VI-5, row 4.

[2] Includes barge rentals which during 1960-64 averaged about $117,000 annually.

A number of points are important for evaluating the above revenue projections.

a. The assumptions made for projecting cargo traffic for the proposed ferry in Chapter III must also be kept in mind in the present case.

b. The 6 per cent compound factor used for the lower projection was also used for projecting cargo estimates for the ferry in Chapter III. The 8 per cent compound factor used for the upper projection is slightly higher than the 7.5 per cent compound rate at which the revenue of the barge time grew annually since 1960.

c. Finally, we assume that the $7 revenue per short ton and the $45 revenue per car will remain unchanged and no substantial improvement of service will take place through 1969.

The percentages of revenue of the barge line which is likely to be diverted to the proposed ferry are shown in row 3 of Table VI-6. A number of points may be helpful for their proper interpretation.

a. For reasons explained earlier the percentages of revenue diversion were obtained by placing the lower and upper revenue projections against the upper and lower revenue diversions, respectively.

b. These percentages of revenue diversion underestimate the magnitude of revenue diversion to the extent to which cash shippers are likely to switch to the proposed ferry.

c. The probable effect of the establishment of the proposed ferry on the barge line is likely to be more severe than the probable effect on the airlines. In the first place, the revenue diversion of cash shippers is likely to increase the percentages of revenue diversion from the barge line above the percentages of revenue diversion from the airlines recorded in row 1c of Table VI-4. In the second place, while the growth of traffic for the barge line is limited, being largely the function of the rate of population and economic growth of the neighboring islands, the growth of air traffic is to an increasing extent a function of the rate of growth of tourist traffic. Presently, 50 per cent of inter-island enplanements are from tourists. By 1969 as much as 70 per cent of enplanements are likely to come from visitors. Furthermore, as far as airlines are concerned, if losses occur they are likely to be met, at least in part, with federal aid. No such opportunity seems to exist for the barge line of Young Brothers, Ltd.

d. Again, for an important decision such as the one on hand it might be advisable to rely on the upper-lower 14.1 per cent of revenue diversion, which represents the worst of the consequences, rather than on the other percentages of revenue diversion.

The "piggyback" method of cargo handling and prospects.--In Chapters III and V we based our analysis on the findings of the cargo survey for the roll-on, roll-off method of handling cargo. Here is the time to explain why we ignored the "piggyback" method before discussing long-run prospects.

155

On one hand, under the "piggyback" method the percentage of revenue diversion to the proposed ferry is likely to be, at a mid-point estimate, 25 percentage points higher than under the roll-on, roll-off method. On the other hand, this method would require the establishment of costly loading and unloading facilities in each port which cannot be justified by the volume such facilities are likely to handle. Furthermore, the use of the proposed ferry as a means of stimulating diversified farming on the neighboring islands seems doubtful. In short, the potential benefits from the proposed ferry as cargo carrier are rather limited and the "piggyback" method of cargo handling is incompatible with the principle of complementarity between carriers. Otherwise, the proposed ferry is likely to be in direct competition with the existing barge line for a volume of traffic which does not seem sufficient for one carrier to enjoy the economies of a large-scale operation.

On the other hand, the "roll-on, roll-off" method of handling cargo seems to be more compatible with the principle of complementarity of service than the "piggyback" method. Also, with respect to the implementation of the proposed ferry, this principle suggests a number of points.

a. It is true that, according to our survey, the service of the barge line may need improvement with respect to frequency, the timely delivery of cargo, the method of handling cargo, and other reasons. However, these reasons are not sufficient to justify the introduction of another carrier which may be designed to duplicate the service given by the barge line. Instead, every effort should be made to encourage the barge line to improve its service.

b. In the long run the establishment of a ferry may generate cargo traffic for the barge line sufficient to offset the initial loss. However, in order to lessen the initial adverse effect of the ferry on the barge line, commercial traffic on the ferry may be restricted. In fact, our earlier suggestion to

exclude commercial traffic altogether during the "trial" period assumes added importance in the light of our present discussion. After all, it is quite possible for the passenger traffic to be quite sufficient so that commercial traffic could be limited and allowed on the ferry on weekdays and during off seasons only.

All told, whether the proposed ferry is conceived as a "toll" road which must pay its own way or a "free" highway, it should be looked upon as a new mode of transportation, supplementing rather than supplanting the existing carriers. If the principle of complementarity is followed, the dislocations which the proposed ferry may initially bring about may be considerably minimized, the period of adjustment for the existing carriers may be shorter, and the ferry may be integrated into the network of existing carriers, giving as well as receiving traffic from other carriers.

THE PROBABLE EFFECT OF THE PROPOSED
FERRY ON THE ECONOMY OF HAWAII

In this chapter, we shall analyze the probable effects which the proposed ferry may have on the Hawaiian economy. Our discussion will be confined to the economic activities generated within the state by the establishment of the ferry and its operation through the first year, that is, 1969. Because of difficulties involved in ascertaining the demand for ferry services beyond its first year of operation, we shall not attempt to make predictions with regard to the economic impact of the ferry after 1969. Instead, we shall build an economic model for the period 1970-1974, based on certain assumptions concerning the ferry's traffic demand and operating costs, which is contained in Chapter IX.

1. Probable Effect on Income and Employment

There are three ways by which the proposed ferry may generate expenditures which, if remaining within the state, will create income and employment. They are: (1) the construction of ferry boats and terminal and harbor facilities; (2) the net addition or reduction in expenditures resulting from the expenditure of the ferry's operating costs and the cutback in spending of the existing inter-island carriers and car rental business; and (3) the added consumption expenditures of people riding the ferry. We shall call them primary net ferry-generated expenditures, to be distinguished from secondary increases in expenditures through the multiplier effect. Once these primary net ferry-generated expenditures are known, then we can compute the expected total increase in expenditures and income through successive rounds of spending.

Primary net ferry-generated expenditures.-- For our analysis of primary net ferry-generated expenditures we shall use only the mid-points of the 1969 revenues and operating costs given in Table V-5 and all the supporting data.

158

We choose the mid-points because we can place more confidence on such points since they are more likely to occur statiscally than either the lower or the upper points. Of course, our procedure could be applied to any combination of revenues and operating costs (lower, mid-point and upper) if the reader deems it desirable to do so. In a similar way, we shall also use the mid-point estimates of capital requirement for the ferry boats and terminal facilities.

The bond issue was discussed in Chapter IV. It is safe to assume that all the bonds will be sold on the U.S. mainland, resulting, therefore, in no investment of local funds in the islands. It may also be assumed that the ferry boats will be built on the mainland while the construction of terminal and harbor facilities will use local labor and some, but not all, local material. The mid-point estimates of capital requirement are $12.6 million for the two boats and $3.8 million for the terminal and harbor facilities (See Table IV-3). The latter is shown in the first section of Table VII-1.

The mid-point first-year operating costs of the proposed ferry were estimated at $4.79 million, which is approximately a break-even point. (See Table V-5 and discussion in Chapter V). But out of the $4.79 million costs, $1.17 will go immediately to the U.S. mainland for debt service charges. Thus, we shall count only the difference, or $3.62 million as a part of the primary net ferry-generated expenditures which would in turn generate expenditures and income within the state.

In assessing the economic impact of the ferry's operation in 1969, however, we must also take into consideration the possible diversion of revenues from the inter-island airlines, the barge line and the car rental firms. In Chapter VI, we discussed the direct effect of the ferry on the operations of the local carriers. Our concern here is the net stimulation to the economy, if any, which will be provided by the ferry. Thus, we need to subtract from the favorable impact of the ferry through the expenditure of its operating costs the negative impact caused by

159

TABLE VII-1

PRIMARY NET FERRY-GENERATED EXPENDITURES
THROUGH FIRST-YEAR OPERATION OF THE FERRY
(Millions of Dollars)

	Total Expenditures	Amount Going to U.S. Mainland Immediately	Primary Net Ferry Generated Expenditures within the State
I. Establishment of ferry			
a. construction of ferry	$12.6	$12.6	0
b. construction of terminal and harbor facilities	3.8		$3.8
Total	$16.4	$12.6	$3.8
II. Operating costs of ferry and ferry-induced cutbacks			
a. operating costs	$ 4.79	$ 1.17	$3.62
b. cutbacks			
local airlines	($ 3.81)	0	($3.81)
barge line	(0.70)	0	(0.70)
car rentals	(0.32)	0	(0.32)
Sub-Total	($ 4.83)	0	($4.83)
Total	($ 0.04)	$ 1.17	($1.21)
III. Additional consumption expenditures			
a. "induced" tourists	$ 0.68	0	$0.68
b. "diverted" tourists	0.40	0	0.40
c. "diverted" state residents	1.65	0	1.65
d. "induced" state residents	5.92	0	5.92
Total	$ 8.65	0	$8.65

loss of revenues to the existing inter-island carriers and car rental business.

Table VI-3 showed that there would be a total diversion of 141,000 round trips from the local airlines consisting of 110,000 trips for state residents and 31,000 for out-of-state tourists. The loss of revenues to the local airlines would be approximately $3.81 million.

Table VI-5 showed that there would be a diversion of revenue of approximately $700,000 from the existing barge line due to loss of cargo and automobile traffic. It was assumed that all the cargo to be carried by the ferry will be a diversion from the barge and that all the automobiles which would have been carried by the barge will go to the ferry after the latter goes into operation.

There is a complete lack of information on possible diversion of business from the car rental operations. We believe, however, that a diversion of 20% of the estimated 45,205 passenger cars to be carried by the ferry in 1969 is not completely out of order. Using the rough figure of 9,000 cars and assuming that the average renter rents it for three days at $12 a day ($8 per day plue 8¢ per mile for 50 miles a day), then the loss of revenue to the car rental business would be approximately $320,000.

Adding them together, the loss of gross revenues to the local airlines, the barge line, and the car rental business will be approximately $4.83 million in the first year of the ferry's operation. It must be stressed here, however, that although the ferry tends to take some business away from them at the beginning, in the long run, through stimulation it will provide to the state's economy, the ferry may promote more travel and business to offset its initial unfavorable effect on these enterprises and be eventually beneficial to them. This has been discussed in Chapter VI. In addition, the $4.83 million figure refers to loss of revenue in 1969. Therefore, all or a large part of this loss of revenue may be offset by growth of their business between 1965 and 1969. Thus, their business in 1969 after

the introduction of the ferry could still be as good as it is now in 1965.

It is doubtful that the inter-island airlines, the barge line, and the car rental firms will reduce their expenditures to the same extent as their expected loss of revenues since a large part of their costs may be fixed. But to be on the conservative side, we shall assume that there will be a cut in their spending amounting to $4.83 million. This is shown in Section II-b of Table VII-1.

Without the benefit of some actual experience, it is difficult to estimate the increase in consumption expenditures of state residents and out-of-state tourists induced by the ferry. The average tourist in Alaska taking the Alaskan Ferry spent, excluding ferry fares, $17 per day in 1963.[1] We shall assume that the tourists in Hawaii who will be attracted to the neighbor islands by the ferry will spend on the average 2.6 days on the neighbor islands, a figure given by the Hawaii Visitors Bureau as the average tourist's actual days of visit on each neighbor island in 1963. In addition, we shall assume, rather arbitrarily, that half of the $44 expenditure per tourist (2.6 days times $17) would otherwise be spent on Oahu, leading to a net increase of $22 per tourist. In other words, we are assuming that those tourists who will go to the neighbor islands as a result of the ferry operation will spend on the average $22 more in the State of Hawaii. Thus, the net induced tourist expendiutre may be estimated at $22 times the number of "induced" tourists, 31,000, or roughly $680,000.

On the other hand, we shall assume that the tourists who will be diverted from the local airlines to go to the neighbor islands by ferry will spend the same amount of money as before. Since they saved about $13 on the transportation cost ($27.00 the average airline fare minus $13.97 the average ferry fare for tourists), this means that they will have an additional $13 dollars per person to spend, either on an extended stay or on some new items of consumption. If our assumptions

[1] Wolf Management Services, Investment Opportunities in Southeastern Alaska, 1964, p. 183.

are considered as reasonable, then the additional spending of "diverted" tourists may be estimated at $13 times 31,000 or approximately $400,000. The loss of revenue to the local airlines will not concern us here since it has already been included as being responsible for cut-backs in expenditures.

In a similar manner, we shall assume that the state residents whose travel to the other islands will be a diversion from the local airlines will spend the same amount as before. This means that they will have roughly an additional $15 ($27.00 minus $12.29, the average ferry fare for the state residents) to spend either on an extended stay or some new items of consumption. Thus, the additional expenditures of "diverted" state residents may be estimated at $15 times 110,000 or approximately $1,650,000.

For the 108,000 passengers or 51,500 households who represent new or induced demand for the ferry, we shall assume that they spend on the average $20 per household per day. This low figure has already taken into consideration the low cost cabins and the fact that many of these people may stay with their relatives. We shall further assume that only $15 of the $20 represent net additional spending since some of the households' regular expenditures at home may be cut as a result of their traveling. Our passenger survey shows that the average households going to the other islands will spend 7.7 days. Using this figure, each household will have about $115 in net additional spending, with a total of $5,920,000 for 51,500 households.

The additional consumption expenditures of people riding the ferry may thus be summarized in Section 3 of Table VII-1.

Only $5.92 million of the $8.05 million additional consumption expenditure will be a net addition to personal consumption by the people of Hawaii. In view of the fact that in 1960, Hawaii's personal savings were $220 million, and that in the same year the people of Hawaii spent $52.9 million traveling in the U.S. Mainland

and abroad,[2] it may not be unreasonable at all to assume that $5.92 million could be diverted from these two sources to local personal consumption in 1969.

The multiplier, a digression.--In order to determine the economic impact of the proposed ferry on income and employment, we need to know the size of the multiplier. This could be computed from the results of a recent study prepared for the Economic Research Center by Dr. Oshima and Mr. Ono.[3] Unfortunately their study does not have any analysis on the multiplier. Neither does it have the data arranged in such a way so that the multiplier is readily computable. At the risk of taxing the readers, we shall reconstruct their data and derive the multiplier. For those readers who do not have interest in this technical subject, it would be advisable to skip this sub-section.

Table VII-2 is mainly definitional. It shows the relationship between the various concepts of state income and gives the steps by which one may be computed from the others. In 1960, for example, out of a total of $2,562.1 million spent in Hawaii on (1) consumption, (2) gross private domestic investment, (3) government purchase of goods and services, and (4) exports, $774.8 million or 30.2 per cent were used to pay imports, resulting in a gross domestic product of $1,787.3 million. The net state income of $1,592.7 million was derived by subtracting depreciation charges ($73.0 million), indirect business taxes ($115.2 million), net factor payments of Hawaii to outsiders ($0.4 million),[4] and business transfers ($6.0 million)[5] from

---

[2]Harry T. Oshima and Mitsuo Ono, Hawaii's Income and Expenditures, 1958, 1959, and 1960. Economic Research Center, University of Hawaii, 1965, p. II-24 and p. II-41. See also our previous discussion in Chapter III, Section 4.

[3]Oshima and Ono, op. cit.

[4]"This is the balance between wages and salaries, interest, dividends and branch profits which were received in Hawaii from the rest of the world and which were paid out from Hawaii to the rest of the world." Oshima and Ono, op. cit., p. II-65.

[5]"This comprises corporate gifts to non-profit institutions and bad debts." Oshima and Ono, op. cit., p. II-60. This item is deducted as a corporate cost from gross domestic product to arrive at the net state income, but added back as a transfer income to come to the state personal income.

164

TABLE VII-2

GROSS DOMESTIC EXPENDITURES AND STATE INCOMES, STATE OF HAWAII, 1958, 1959, and 1960
(Millions of Dollars)

	1960		1959		1958	
Gross Domestic Expenditures		2,562.1		2,270.2		2,007.0
Less: Imports		774.8		704.5		624.7
Gross Domestic Product		1,787.3		1,565.7		1,382.3
Less: Net Factor Payments Abroad		0.4		11.7		9.6
Depreciation		73.0		71.0		59.0
Business Transfers		6.0		5.0		4.0
Indirect Business Taxes						
State and local	111.5		99.7		86.9	
Federal	3.7	115.2	4.4	104.1	0.1	87.0
Net State Income		1,592.7		1,373.9		1,222.7
Less: Corporate Taxes						
State and local	5.7		5.1		7.6	
Federal	42.1	47.8	36.1	41.2	32.2	39.8
Undistributed Profits		122.0		77.0		56.0
Employers' Contribution for Social Insurance						
State and local	5.0		3.9		3.2	
Federal	0.9	5.9	0.8	4.7	0.7	3.9
Plus: Government Interest						
State and local	5.7		5.3		3.8	
Federal	3.7	9.4	2.4	7.7	1.8	5.6
Other Government Transfer						
State and local	20.2		17.8		15.4	
Federal	39.0	59.2	37.8	55.6	33.6	49.0
Business Transfers		6.0		5.0		4.0
Unilateral External Account Transfers		22.8		13.1		3.7
State Personal Income		1,514.4		1,332.4		1,185.3
Less: Personal Taxes						
State and local	54.3		57.5		36.9	
Federal	186.5	240.8	158.2	215.7	137.4	174.3
State Disposable Income		1,273.6		1,116.7		1,011.0
Less: Personal Savings		220.3		149.3		145.2
Personal Consumption		1,053.3		967.4		865.8

Source: Computed from Oshima and Ono, op. cit., Chapter II

the gross domestic product of 1960. The derivations of state personal income and state disposable income could be traced in a similar manner. They need not be elaborated here.

In Table VII-3, the information contained in Table VII-2, is further grouped into certain categories and expressed as a percentage of the gross domestic expenditures. The average percentages for the three years 1958, 1959 and 1960 are presented in the last column of the table.

From Table VII-3, it can be seen that out of the gross domestic expenditures, certain portions go to imports, depreciation, taxes, etc. In 1960, for example, 30.2% of the gross domestic output went to imports, 2.9% to depreciation, 6.9% to state and local taxes, 9.1% to federal taxes, 4.8% to undistributed profits. Then there were 3.6% government and unilateral external account transfers, giving us a state disposable income which was 49.7% of the gross domestic expenditures. Personal savings were 8.6% of the gross domestic expenditures in 1960 while personal consumption was 41.1%. It must be cautioned here that according to the definition used in the Oshima-Ono report, this personal consumption includes consumption of both domestic and imported goods and services.

If we take the average percentages of these shares for the three years 1958, 1959 and 1960, and assume that these same percentages will apply to 1969 and beyond, then we may use them for determining the multiplier. In so doing, we are not only assuming that the percentages will remain the same over the years, but also that the ratio of incremental changes are the same as the averages. For example, if we assume that imports will remain as 30.8% of the gross domestic expenditures, then the ratio of the increase in imports over any increase in gross domestic expenditures must also be 30.8%. We are well aware of the fact that as income increases the share of income going to consumption will decline and that imports, taxes, etc. as a percentage of gross domestic expenditures will change over a period of time. But the

the gross domestic product of 1960. The definitions of state personal income and state disposable income could be treated in a similar manner. They need not be elaborated here.

In Table VII-3, the information contained in Table VII-... is further grouped into certain categories and expressed as a percentage of the gross domestic expenditures. The average percentage for the three years 1950, 1955 and 1960 are presented in the last column of the table.

From Table VII-3, it can be seen that out of the gross domestic expenditures, certain portions go to imports, depreciation, taxes, etc. In 1960, for example, 50.2% of the gross domestic output went to imports, 7.5% to depreciation, 6.9% to state and local taxes, 9.7% to federal taxes, 8.8% to undistributed profits. Then there were 5.6% government and unilateral external account, giving us a state disposable income which was ... of the gross domestic expenditures. Personal ... were 5.6% of the gross domestic expenditures in 1960 while personal consumption was 61.1%. It must be cautioned here that according to the definition used in the ECAFE report, this personal consumption included consumption of both domestic and imported goods and services.

If we take the average percentages of these shares for the three years 1950, 1955 and 1960, and assume that these same percentages will apply to 1961 and beyond, then we may use them for determining the multiplier. In so doing we are not only assuming that the percentages will remain the same over the years, but also that the ... of increments changes are the same as the averages. For example, if we assume that imports will remain at 50.2% of the gross domestic expenditures, then the ratio of the increase in imports over any increase in gross domestic expenditures must also be 50.2%. ... it ... will mean that, as income increases the share of ... going to consumption will decline and that imports, taxes, etc. as a per cent of gross domestic expenditures will change over a period of time, but the

166

TABLE VII-3

PERCENTAGE DISTRIBUTION OF GROSS DOMESTIC EXPENDITURES IN MODIFIED GROUPING,
STATE OF HAWAII, 1958, 1959 and 1960

	1960 (million dollars)	Per Cent	1959 (million dollars)	Per Cent	1958 (million dollars)	Per Cent	Average Per Cent of 3 Yrs.
Gross Domestic Expenditures	2,562.1	100	2,270.2	100	2,007.0	100	100
Less: Imports	774.8	30.2	704.5	31.0	624.7	31.1	30.8
Gross Domestic Product	1,787.3	69.8	1,565.7	69.0	1,382.3	68.9	69.2
Less: Depreciation	73.0	2.9	71.0	3.1	59.0	2.9	3.0
Net Factor Payment Abroad	0.4	--	11.7	0.5	9.6	0.5	0.3
State and Local Taxes	176.5	6.9	166.2	7.3	134.6	6.7	7.0
Federal Taxes	233.2	9.1	199.5	8.8	170.0	8.5	8.8
Undistributed Profits	122.0	4.8	77.0	3.4	56.0	2.8	3.7
Add: State and Local Gov't. Interest and Transfers	25.9	1.0	23.1	1.0	19.2	1.0	1.0
Federal Gov't. Interest and Transfers	42.7	1.7	40.2	1.8	35.4	1.8	1.8
Unilateral External Account Transfers	22.8	0.9	13.1	0.6	3.7	0.2	0.6
State Disposable Income	1,273.6	49.7	1,116.7	49.2	1,011.0	50.3	49.7
Less: Personal Savings	220.3	8.6	149.3	6.6	145.2	7.2	7.5
Personal Consumption	1,053.3	41.1	967.4	42.6	865.8	43.1	42.3
Net State Income	1,592.7	62.2	1,373.9	60.5	1,222.7	60.9	61.2
State Personal Income	1,514.4	59.1	1,332.4	58.7	1,185.3	59.1	59.0

Source: Computed from Table VII-2.

Note: Individual parts do not add up to total because of rounding.

number of years for which detailed statistics are available is too few and the statistics we do have for these years are too crude[6] to warrant a more refined study. In spite of these limitations, however, we believe that the predictions based on a multiplier so constructed will be sufficient for practical usage. They will offer useful guidelines to decision makers.

We may now proceed to construct the expenditure multiplier utilizing the data in the last column of Table VII-3.

Let: E = gross domestic expenditures

M = imports

Yg = gross domestic product

Yn = net state income

Yp = state personal income

Yd = state disposable income

C = personal consumption

Δ = an affix to indicate an incremental (or decremental) change

A = any autonomous increase in expenditures

And given that:

$$\frac{\Delta M}{\Delta E} = \frac{M}{E} = 30.8\%$$

$$\frac{\Delta Y_g}{\Delta E} = \frac{Y_g}{E} = 1 - \frac{\Delta M}{\Delta E} = 69.2\%$$

$$\frac{\Delta Y_n}{\Delta E} = \frac{Y_n}{E} = 61.2\%$$

$$\frac{\Delta Y_p}{\Delta E} = \frac{Y_p}{E} = 59.0\%$$

$$\frac{\Delta Y_d}{\Delta E} = \frac{Y_d}{E} = 49.7\%$$

$$\frac{\Delta C}{\Delta E} = \frac{C}{E} = 42.3\%$$

---

[6]See, for example, Dr. Oshima's preface to Oshima and Ono, op. cit.

168

Then: $\quad \Delta E = A + \Delta C = A + \dfrac{\Delta C}{\Delta E} \cdot \Delta E = A + 0.423\ \Delta E$

or: $\quad \Delta E\ (1 - 0.423) = A$

or: $\quad \Delta E = \dfrac{1}{1 - 0.423}\ A = \dfrac{1}{0.577}\ A = 1.733\ A$

And: $\quad \Delta Yg = 0.692\ \Delta E = 0.692 \times 1.733\ A$
$\qquad\qquad\quad = 1.199\ A$

$\quad\qquad \Delta Yn = 0.612\ \Delta E = 1.061\ A$

$\quad\qquad \Delta Yp = 0.59\ \Delta E = 1.023\ A$

$\quad\qquad \Delta Yd = 0.498\ \Delta E = 0.861\ A$

In other words, a $1,000,000 autonomous increase in expenditures will cause gross domestic expenditures to rise by $1,733,000. The expenditure multiplier is 1.733. Likewise, a $1,000,000 autonomous increase in expenditures will raise gross domestic product by $1,199,000, net state income by $1,061,000, state personal income by $1,023,000, and state disposable income by $861,000. The value of the multiplier differs according to which concept of the state income one uses.[7]

Expected multiplier effect on income and employment.--In this study we shall adopt the same multiplier for all types of expenditures. Although it is true that in a small state like Hawaii, where imports play an eminent role, it may be more meaningful to use sectoral multipliers which are different mainly because of different propensities to import, our time and budget do not allow us to make first-hand research in this area. Unfortunately, we find the information contained in The Impact of Exports on Income in Hawaii prepared by

---

[7]Our concept of expenditure multiplier differs from the concept of income multiplier in The Impact of Exports on Income in Hawaii, Department of Economic Research, First National Bank of Hawaii. It is only by coincidence that the figures are practically the same.

the Department of Economic Research of the First National Bank of Hawaii not suitable for our use. This is mainly because its "local income" created by different types of expenditures lumps together all the elements of gross domestic product except federal taxes and other out-payments while its multiplier should apply only to personal income.[8] It will require considerable amount of time and work to desegregate the various elements of "local income" if it is possible to do so at all. Besides, only expenditures relative to consumption and export industries are covered in that report. Many types of expenditures which we need for our study are not included there.

We also regret that we cannot make use of the input-output tables of the forthcoming Oahu Transportation Study primarily because they took a number of short cuts in estimating inter-industry demand, thus minimizing their usefulness to our study. Furthermore, the Oahu Transportation Study is still in its semi-finished stage and needs certain check-up and revision. Lastly, it applies only to the island of Oahu. Work is required to expand it to cover the whole state.

Applying the information contained in the last sub-section on multiplier and in Table VII-1 on primary net ferry-generated spending through 1969, we may estimate the expected total increase in expenditures and income through successive rounds of spending. The results are presented in Table VII-4, with explanations to follow.

The $3.8 million expenditure on construction of terminal and harbor facilities will be spent partly on local labor and material. The other part will go to the U.S. Mainland via import. Since we do not use the sectoral multiplier,

---

[8]See for example, pp. 21-25, op. cit.

170

TABLE VII-4

EXPECTED MULTIPLIER EFFECT ON EXPENDITURES AND
INCOME RESULTED FROM PRIMARY FERRY-GENERATED EXPENDITURES
THROUGH FIRST-YEAR OF FERRY OPERATION ($ Million)

	Net Primary Ferry-Generated Expenditures	Expected Increase in Gross Domestic Expenditures (Multiplier =1.733)	Expected Increase in Gross Domestic Product (Multiplier =1.199)	Expected Increase in State Personal Income (Multiplier =1.023)	Year in Whole Bulk of Impact Will Be Felt
I. Construction of terminal and harbor facilities	$3.8	$6.6	$4.6	$3.9	1969
II. Operating costs and ferry-induced cutbacks	($1.21)	($ 2.1)	($ 1.5)	($1.2)	1970
III. Additional consumption expenditures	$8.65	$15.0	$10.4	$8.9	1970

we assume that like the state average, 30.8% of this expenditure will be sent to the mainland, resulting in a gross domestic expenditure of $2.6 million ($3.8 million x 69.2%) and a personal consumption of $1.6 million ($3.8 million x 42.3%). This second-round consumption spending will add $1.6 million to gross domestic expenditures, $1.1 million to gross domestic product and a personal consumption of $0.7 million which will start the third-round of increase in personal consumption, etc. It is believed that the bulk of this expected expansion of $6.6 million in gross domestic expenditures, $4.6 million in gross domestic product and $3.9 million in state personal income will be felt before the end of the year following the completion of the construction project, namely 1969. (See Table VII-4.)

Applying similar procedures, we find that there will be a net expected drop in gross domestic expenditures by $2.1 million, in gross domestic product by $1.5 million and in state personal income by $1.2 million due to the spending of the ferry's operating costs in 1969 and the cutback in expenditures of the existing inter-island carriers and of the car rental firms. On the other hand, the added expenditures of state residents and out-of-state tourists to be induced by the ferry will result in an expected increase in gross domestic expenditures by $15.0 million, in gross domestic product by $10.4 million and in state personal income by $8.9 million. (See Table VII-4.) It is believed that the bulk of these impacts will be felt before the end of 1970.

Strictly speaking, the initial increase in consumption by state residents as a result of the ferry would alter the consumption function. But since the amount involved is only about half of one per cent of consumption in 1960, and our estimates are very crude to start with, we shall ignore this complication.

If we accept that the construction of the terminal facilities will result in an increase in state personal income of $3.9 million, and if we take $5,700

as the average annual salary of a worker,[9] then the $3.9 million will provide almost 700 jobs for one year.

Likewise, if we accept that there will be a net increase in state personal income of $7.7 million ($8.9 million - $1.2 million) because of the ferry's first-year operation then there will be additional employment of about 1,350 for one year.

We have projected here only the direct impact of the ferry on the Hawaiian economy in terms of expenditures and income. There may also be indirect impact through the effects of ferry operations on balance of trade, capital investment, etc. which we will turn to in the next two sections.

2. Possible Economic Impact on Hawaii's Balance of Payment

In view of the many imponderables involved and the lack of satisfactory detailed trade and other data, no estimates can be made of the effect a ferry system might have on Hawaii's current account with overseas areas.

Tourism.--An inter-island ferry system could be a factor in increased expenditures by overseas visitors in Hawaii, especially if the existence of a ferry is vigorously promoted. The increase could result in two ways by encouraging more tourists to come to the Islands and also by lengthening the average stay here. Even though the ferry system is not intended especially for out-of-state tourists, the Hawaii Visitors Bureau could vigorously use its existence in its promotion of travel to the islands. The key aspect is not only whether large numbers of out-of-state visitors would use a ferry, but also whether it could be used to induce more tourists to come to Hawaii and lengthen their stay especially during the off-season.

---

[9]According to the Research Division of the State Department of Labor, the average annual salary of public and private employees in the State of Hawaii is currently $4,865. Allowing a compound rate of increase of 4% a year, the expected salary in 1969 would be $5,700.

173

Exports to U.S. Mainland.--A ferry system is likely to have little effect on either import or export trade with foreign countries. With respect to trade with the Mainland import substitution appears more promising than export expansion. Sugar and pineapple exports have accounted for almost 90 per cent of the exports of the islands and a ferry system is not likely to have any effect on these products. Other exports, although still quite small, especially fish products, papaya, other tropical fruits, and macadamia nuts have been growing during the last few years. After suffering a sharp decline, Kona coffee exports have also recovered to some extent. However, these exports are not likely to be affected by the proposed ferry.

Import substitution - Manufactured goods.--In examining the possibilities of import substitution, we have to consider that finished manufactures and manufactured foodstuffs comprise the major part of the state's imports. According to a forthcoming Economic Research Center study, finished manufactures comprised about 72 per cent and manufactured foodstuffs about 15 per cent of total imports of the state from overseas areas in 1961; on the other hand, crude foodstuffs comprised about 5 per cent of the state's total imports in 1961.[10] Therefore, the greatest possibilities for import substitution appear to be in manufacturing. However, there is little that a ferry system can do to directly encourage manufacturing in the state to replace imports. Most manufacturing and the market for its products are concentrated in Oahu. Moreover, there is little in the way of an economic base for establishing manufacturing in the neighbor islands.

Import substitution - Agricultural products.--Basically there are two ways in which a ferry system could foster local production of agricultural commodities

_____

[10]Ronald Graybeal, unpublished study on Hawaii's External Trade.

to replace imports. One way would be to provide farmers with a more satisfactory, more frequent, and more efficient service to ship produce for sale in the Honolulu market. Second, a ferry might bring large numbers of people to the neighbor islands to consume locally produced farm products.

During the last decade, Hawaii has not made much progress in supplying most diversified agricultural products from local production. As we can see in Table VII-5, producers in the state supplied an average of 45 per cent of the Honolulu market supply of fruits and vegetables in the years 1960 to 1963, compared to an average of 43 per cent in the years 1950 to 1953. On the other hand, there has been a pronounced tendency for local farmers to supply a much higher proportion of the Honolulu market supply of eggs and chickens.

However, we should also emphasize that a great deal of the Honolulu market supply of key agricultural products has come from Oahu farmers. Farmers in Oahu grow most or substantial proportions of the state's production of eggs, chickens, snap beans, broccoli, sweet corn, lettuce, peppers, watermelons, bananas, cucumbers and a number of other products. On the other hand, farmers on the neighbor islands grow a major part of the state's production of tomatoes, cabbage, carrots, celery, pumpkins, tangerines, and several other diversified crops.

In general, we find two key aspects to the Honolulu market supply. First, well over half of the Honolulu market supply of diversified vegetables and fruits is supplied by mainland production. Second, Oahu farmers continue to raise major part of the state's production of many vegetables and fruits.

As shown in Table VII-6, the average acre devoted to vegetables and melon production and the number of commercial farms of this type in the state have declined sharply over the last decade. The cash receipts from marketing vegetables and melons have increased somewhat, even though the acreage and number of farms have

175

TABLE VII-5

STATE SUPPLY OF SELECTED FRUITS, VEGETABLES, EGGS, CHICKENS, AND MEAT
AS A PERCENTAGE OF TOTAL HONOLULU MARKET SUPPLY FOR SELECTED YEARS

	1950	1951	1952	1953	1960	1961	1962	1963
				(Per Cent)				
Specified fruits and vegetables, fresh	43	37	47	45	45	46	47	40
Eggs, shell	61	57	61	63	82	85	86	90
Chickens	27	30	36	46	42	40	41	40
Beef and veal	52	68	60	43	46	43	46	42
Pork	58	54	58	64	52	45	41	37
Lamb and mutton	6	3	11	7	3	1	2	2
Total red meats	53	61	58	49	47	43	43	40

Sources: U.S. Department of Agriculture, Agricultural Marketing Service and Hawaii Department of Agriculture, Cooperating, Honolulu Unloads; Fruits, Vegetables, Meats, Dairy and Poultry Products, 1959-1963 from 1963 edition, pp. 6-7 and 1950-1953 from 1954 edition, pp. 4-5.

176

TABLE VII-6

CROP ACRES, NUMBER OF COMMERCIAL SIZE FARMS, AND CASH RECEIPTS FROM MARKETINGS DIVERSIFIED VEGETABLES AND FRUITS FOR SELECTED YEARS

	Crop Acres		Number of Commercial Size Farms[1]		Cash Receipts from Marketings	
	Vegetables and Melons	Fruits	Vegetables and Melons	Fruits	Vegetables and Melons	Fruits
1954	4,300	1,840	1,262[2]	667[2]	3,917	1,148
1955	4,440	1,770	1,066[2]	744[2]	4,191	1,209
1956	4,290	2,000	826	983	4,384	1,255
1957	4,010	2,160	293	283	4,377	1,278
1958	3,760	2,160	780	765	4,643	1,390
1959	3,620	2,190	773	786	4,355	1,324
1960	3,440	2,240	762	809	4,577	1,315
1961	3,420	2,350	786	806	4,809	1,653
1962	3,280	2,340	730	809	4,897	1,488
1963	3,160	2,390	744	818	4,774	1,720

[1] The number of commercial size farms on January 1 of the following year.

[2] Melons included with fruits for 1954 and 1955.

Source: Hawaii Crop and Livestock Reporting Service, Statistics of Hawaii Agriculture, 1963, pp. 708 and 16.

declined. This probably indicated that the more efficient farms have continued operations. On the other hand, the number of acres devoted to diversified fruits production, the number of commercial fruit farms, and the cash receipts from marketing fruits have grown in the last decade. Thus, there may have been some shift from vegetable to fruit production. However, diversified fruits produced in Hawaii are primarily tropical ones, in which the state has absolute advantages and which are not competitive with mainland production. It is also significant to note, as we see in Table VII-7, that over one-third of crop acres in vegetable and melon production and almost one-third of acreage devoted to fruit production in the state in 1963 were in Oahu. Thus the record over the last decade is not especially encouraging with respect to local production of diversified vegetables and fruits on the neighbor islands to replace imports, unless some major structural changes take place.

The reasons why local production and especially why neighbor island farmers have not been able to supply more of the State's requirements of diversified farm products have been discussed in many reports and is beyond the scope of this study.[10] Yet, we may point out some factors involved. Farmers in the state do have one advantage, lower transportation costs than mainland farmers in supplying local requirements, but this has not been enough. Most diversified farms in the state are small, often family operations. With a small scale

---

[10]See J. A. Mollett, Hawaii's Future Agriculture, December 1962; Cost of Producing Lettuce in Hawaii, July 1961; Cost of Producing Tomatoes in Hawaii, January 1963; Cost of Producing Celery in Hawaii, June 1963. Douglas J. McConnell, Molokai Demonstration Farm Project, April 1963. C. W. Peters and John L. Rasmussen, Integrating Hawaiian Agriculture Through Cooperatives, December 1961. All published by College of Tropical Agriculture, University of Hawaii. Hawaii Farm Bureau Federation, A Study of the Economic and Technical Feasibility of the Establishment of a Vacuum Cooling Plant on Maui, December 1961.

TABLE VII-7

CROP ACRES FOR DIVERSIFIED VEGETABLES AND FRUITS
BY MAJOR ISLANDS, 1963

	Vegetables and Melons		Fruits	
	Acres	Per Cent of Total	Acres	Per Cent of Total
Oahu	1,140	36	750	31
Hawaii	1,060	34	1,270	53
Maui	840	27	170	7
Kauai	110	3	200	8
Molokai	10	1/	5	1/
Total	3,160	100	2,390 2/	100

1/ Less than 0.5 per cent.

2/ Components do not add to total in source.

Source: Hawaii Crop and Livestock Reporting Service, Statistics of Hawaii Agriculture, 1963, p. 7.

TABLE VIII.

CROP ACRES FOR DESIGNATED VEGETABLE AND FRUITS
BY MAJOR ISLANDS, 1961

	Vegetables and Melons		Fruits	
	Acres	Per cent of Total	Acres	Per cent of Total
Oahu	1,160 2/	35	750	31
Hawaii	1,660	34	1,270	53
Maui	800	17	170	7
Kauai	110	3	200	8
Molokai	110	1/	2/	1/
Total	3,130	100	2,390 2/	100

1/ Less than 0.5 per cent.

2/ Components do not add to total in source.

Source: Hawaii Crop and Livestock Reporting Service, Statistics of Hawaii Agriculture, 1962, p. 7.

production, not always up to date production and processing techniques and ineffective marketing, local farmers have been faced with high unit costs. Many produce men point to ineffective handling, refrigeration, grading, packing, excessive spoilage and in some cases poor quality of locally produced farm products. They also point to the fact that local supply is often unreliable and due to the existence of a pocket market in Hawaii it is difficult to dispose of farm products, when there is excess supply. There is also a movement away from farming to other occupations. On the other hand, farmers on the mainland have had large scale units, used more mechanization and more effective production techniques, in some cases have used cheaper Mexican labor, and have been better organized in marketing their products.

Our analysis, therefore, indicates that an inter-island sea ferry is not likely to have significant effects in import substitution of diversified vegetables and fruits, unless there are major structural changes in the agricultural production, marketing, including probably the more systematic development of cooperatives. Inadequate as is the present method of inter-island surface transportation for handling produce, it does not seem primarily responsible for the failure of local farmers to supply more of the state's requirements of agricultural products.

The second way in which a ferry system can encourage import substitution is by bringing large numbers of people from Oahu to the neighbor islands. In many respects, this seems to be more promising. Once again there are the problems of local farmers producing and effectively marketing their products to hotels, restaurants, and stores providing food products to state residents and out-of-state visitors. These problems do not appear to be as complicated as marketing farm products in the Honolulu market. At least, potential exists for expansion in production, because of available land and other factors to

supply local requirements of many farm products. If local farmers can supply visitors' demand for food products, then they may be in a better position to organize more effectively to supply the Honolulu market. On the other hand, the greater supply of farm products to visitors to the neighbor islands could also divert supplies of produce away from the Honolulu market.

To the extent that the ferry would cause an import substitution, the propensity to import for the state would change. So would the multipliers. But since the substitution is not likely to be large, and since it is extremely difficult to quantify, we did not introduce this factor into our multiplier analysis.

3. Other Probable Economic Effects

Possible economic impact on the value of land and capital investment.--It is difficult to predict quantitatively the effect of the ferry on land value. In general, it can be said that with the stimulation which it will provide to the economy of the neighbor islands, the ferry will tend to increase the land value there. And to the extent that the ferry will move tourists and Oahu residents to the neighbor islands, it will tend to reduce the pressure on land in Oahu. But as pointed out earlier, the ferry alone is not likely to result in a migration of industries to the neighbor islands or a great expansion of agricultural activities. Some structural changes must take place to provide the neighbor islands with greater comparative advantages in order to result in significant migration or expansion.

The ferry will also tend to raise land value in the neighbor islands through more demand for sites for drive-in restaurants, service stations, low-priced hotels, cabins and cottages, and general facilities for recreation.

181

The experience of the Southeastern Alaskan Ferry shows that the ferry has contributed to an increase in investment and in businessmen's interest in Southeastern Alaska. However, most of the investment to date has been in tourist accomodations and related facilities. There is some concern in Alaska about whether tourist facilities are worthwhile investments. This is because the tourist season in Alaska is very short, leaving most of the facilities unoccupied during eight or nine months of the year.[11] Fortunately, Hawaii's weather allows year-round vacationing. This will make investment in tourist accommodations and related facilities more attractive, although seasonal fluctuations in business are still unavoidable.

There may also be some added investment in diversified agriculture induced by the ferry, but the magnitude is likely to be limited.

It is impossible to estimate at this moment the amount of capital investment to be induced by the proposed ferry. It is therefore not practical to predict the increase in state income to be caused by the induced capital investments. Suffice it to say here that the multiplier effect will apply equally to induced investment expenditures.

Possible economic impact on state and local taxes.--The increase in expenditures by tourists and state residents to be induced by the ferry will result in higher collection of state and local taxes. First, the state will collect and share with the counties the 3½% sales tax and the ½% general excise tax. Second, the state will collect more income taxes from individuals and corporations as their income rises. Third, gasoline tax revenues to the state and county will increase with more people traveling. Fourth, collection of

[11]Wolf Management Services, Investment Opportunities in Southeastern Alaska, op. cit., p. 4.

real property taxes may rise with rising land value in the neighbor islands,
providing these counties with more revenues. Lastly, there are other minor
taxes which will also increase with higher expenditures. In all, if we apply
the 7% average of state and local taxes to gross domestic expenditures in
Table VII-3, there might be a total increase of $460,000 in state and local
taxes because of the terminal and harbor construction ($3.8 million x 1.733
x 7%) and of $900,000 ($12.9 million x 7%) because of the first-year operation
of the ferry.

The probable effect of the proposed ferry system on tourism and on the
existing local carriers has already been examined in earlier chapters.

CHAPTER VIII

ECONOMIC DEVELOPMENT OF NEIGHBOR ISLANDS

1. General Background

It is well known that economic growth of the Hawaiian economy since 1950 has been primarily concentrated on Oahu. With less than one-tenth of the land area of the state, Oahu has over 80 per cent the total population and a pre-dominance of economic activity in the state.[1] During the last decade it has increased its economic predominance with a rapid economic growth, while there has been a slow rate of growth on the other islands. As Table VIII-1 shows, major economic indicators--population, employment, personal income per capita, retail sales, construction, and others--conclusively show the lag in economic development in the neighbor islands. Thus, a kind of economic dualism has developed with rapid growth in income and production on Oahu and near economic stagnation on the neighbor islands. One has only to travel widely in the state to see the striking disparity in incomes, standards of living, and development between Oahu and the other islands.

What has held back the economic growth of the neighbor islands? What can be done to encourage greater development in the other islands in the future? What part can an inter-island ferry system play in their economic growth?

While a comprehensive analysis of these questions is beyond the scope of this study, we do want to point out certain aspects of the problem. Many factors are involved in development including quantity and quality of the labor force, deepening and widening of capital investments, development and application of technology, business enterprise, extent of the market and consumer demand,

---

[1] See Bank of Hawaii, Department of Business Research, Annual Economic Reports, 1963 and 1964.

184

TABLE VIII-1

ECONOMIC INDICATORS BY COUNTIES
(1950, 1953, 1962 and 1963)

	1950		1953		1962		1963	
	Total	Per cent of State Total	Total	Per cent of State Total	Total	Per cent of State Total	Total	Per cent of State Total
Oahu								
Population (as of July 1)	324,768	68.7	329,078	70.3	501,356	78.8	520,999	79.5
Civilian Labor Force	131,876	70.2	139,675	71.2	195,260	79.3	199,140	79.4
Employment	119,369	70.2	132,458	71.0	186,140	79.3	189,810	79.5
Unemployment	12,507	70.7	7,217	75.6	9,120	78.6	9,330	77.6
Unemployment Rate (Per cent)	9.5		5.2		4.7		4.7	
Per Capita Personal Income (Dollars)	1,534		2,194		2,546		2,604	
Value of Diversified Agriculture (1,000 dollars)	12,886	45.0	17,367	50.4	22,372	51.3	21,909	49.0
Acres in Cultivation	4,324	29.4	3,700	27.4	2,180	14.0	2,060	13.2
Retail Trade (1,000 dollars)	399,932	83.2	456,223	84.3	783,987	85.1	791,785	85.2
Construction (1,000 dollars)	60,177	88.9	88,162	91.0	232,883	90.6	242,528	91.4
Manufacturing (1,000 dollars)	57,697	88.9	86,169	87.4	145,226	91.8	154,274	90.5
Hawaii								
Population (as of July 1)	68,883	14.6	63,565	13.6	60,246	9.5	60,649	9.3
Civilian Labor Force	24,922	13.3	24,955	12.7	22,240	9.0	22,400	8.9
Employment	22,384	13.2	23,877	12.8	21,330	9.1	21,370	8.9
Unemployment	2,538	14.3	1,078	11.3	910	7.8	1,030	8.6
Unemployment Rate (Per cent)	10.2		4.3		4.1		4.6	
Per Capita Personal Income (Dollars)	1,031		1,196		1,830		1,950	
Value of Diversified Agriculture (1,000 dollars)	9,839	34.3	11,697	33.9	12,735	29.2	14,691	32.8
Acres in Cultivation	6,856	46.5	7,200	53.3	11,140	71.6	11,550	74.4
Retail Trade (1,000 dollars)	40,068	8.4	42,189	7.8	63,185	6.9	63,621	6.9
Construction (1,000 dollars)	4,920	7.3	4,530	4.7	12,192	4.7	11,247	4.2
Manufacturing (1,000 dollars)	5,639	8.7	10,778	10.9	8,007	5.1	9,434	5.5

185

TABLE VIII-1--Continued

	1950		1953		1962		1963	
	Total	Per cent of State Total	Total	Per cent of State Total	Total	Per cent of State Total	Total	Per cent of State Total
Maui								
Population (as of July 1)	48,839	10.3	45,756	9.8	45,625	7.2	45,916	7.0
Civilian Labor Force	18,596	9.9	18,613	9.5	17,090	6.9	17,470	7.0
Employment	16,678	9.8	17,843	9.6	16,090	6.9	16,440	6.9
Unemployment	1,918	10.8	770	8.1	1,000	8.6	1,030	8.6
Unemployment Rate (Per cent)	10.3		4.1		5.8		5.9	
Per Capita Personal Income (Dollars)	1,131		1,224		1,733		1,978	
Value of Diversified Agriculture (1,000 dollars)	4,137	14.4	3,679	10.7	5,267	12.1	5,138	11.5
Acres in Cultivation	2,617	17.8	1,700	12.6	1,584	10.2	1,294	8.3
Retail Trade (1,000 dollars)	24,629	5.1	25,588	4.7	43,043	4.7	43,514	4.7
Construction (1,000 dollars)	1,236	1.8	2,042	2.1	7,680	3.0	6,869	2.6
Manufacturing (1,000 dollars)	980	1.5	1,111	1.1	3,418	2.2	4,578	2.7
Kauai								
Population (as of July 1)	30,290	6.4	29,902	6.4	28,661	4.5	27,982	4.3
Civilian Labor Force	12,379	6.6	12,898	6.6	11,590	4.7	11,880	4.7
Employment	11,644	6.9	12,422	6.7	11,020	4.7	11,250	4.7
Unemployment	735	4.2	476	5.0	570	4.9	630	5.2
Unemployment Rate (Per cent)	5.9		3.7		4.9		5.3	
Per Capita Personal Income (Dollars)	1,142		1,204		1,964		2,250	
Value of Diversified Agriculture (1,000 dollars)	1,795	6.3	1,734	5.0	3,260	7.5	3,009	6.7
Acres in Cultivation	934	6.3	900	6.7	650	4.2	630	4.1
Retail Trade (1,000 dollars)	15,843	3.3	17,293	3.2	30,743	3.3	29,975	3.2
Construction (1,000 dollars)	1,377	2.0	2,171	2.2	4,197	1.6	4,579	1.7
Manufacturing (1,000 dollars)	559	0.9	517	0.5	1,506	0.9	2,215	1.3

Sources: Hawaii State Department of Health
Hawaii State Department of Labor and Industrial Relations
Tax Commissioner of Hawaii, Annual Reports
Hawaii Crop and Livestock Reporting Service, Statistics of Hawaiian Agriculture
Tax Foundation, Government of Hawaii
First National Bank of Hawaii

social overhead expenditures on education and health, transportation, communications, power, water and other natural resources, and government environment. Inadequacy in many of these vital ingredients have held back growth of the neighbor islands. Also, the concentration on sugar and pineapple, the predominance of rural communities, the systems of land tenure, and the isolation of the neighbor islands have contributed to relatively slow economic growth. As in many other parts of the United States, commerce, finance, manufacturing, construction and other economic activities have been concentrated in the urban core located in Honolulu and surrounding areas in Oahu; these economic activities have developed rather slowly in the outlying, more rural and isolated areas located in the other islands. The neighbor islands have experienced vicious circles characteristic of less developed areas. The small population has meant limited markets, which have held down savings, investments, and economic expansion. The small markets have also meant that any production has operated at a small, often uneconomical scale. With limited opportunities and stagnating economies, workers, capital, technology, and business enterprise have tended to move to and concentrate in Oahu.

Urbanization, social and economic overhead investments, especially education, and technological advances--all of which are keys to economic growth and give it momentum--have been concentrated in Oahu. This does not mean that the neighbor islands have not had their share of governmental expenditures on education, public health, highways, airports, sea ports, and other intra-structure as well as private development of power and communications. The record shows that, on a per capita basis, they may have had more than Oahu. In fact, there has probably been some redistribution of income through governmental expenditures from Oahu to the other islands. Yet, in view of the relatively large areas involved, the small populations, and the rural character of the communities, social and economic

overhead capital could not be provided as effectively either quantitatively or
qualitatively on the neighbor islands as on Oahu. As a result the neighbor
islands have lagged in many respects in their economic development.

We do not claim that this is a complete picture of such a complex process as
inter-island growth, but it does broadly sketch some factors involved. We should
also stress that development is a process involving many inter-actions of basic
ingredients. Once the process of growth starts, there may be many feedbacks and
interactions that accentuate growth. Tourism may be considered a leading sector
in the growth of Oahu in recent years, but it has also encouraged considerable
construction, manufacturing, agricultural production, finance and service activities in the Honolulu area. Now there are signs that the neighbor islands,
especially Maui, have started to turn the corner toward more rapid development.
Tourism may be considered the leading sector in the improved outlook for the
neighbor islands. Perhaps an inter-island ferry system, by transporting large
numbers of local residents to the neighbor islands, can also contribute to their
development along with the out-of-state visitor industry.

2. General Economic Development Aspects of a Ferry System

In the previous chapters we have considered the possible impact of a ferry
system on personal income, investments, external trade, and tourism. A great
deal of this economic impact would be felt in the neighbor islands. The crucial
factor that we have pointed out would be the extent of increased travel by island
residents, and to a lesser extent out-of-state visitors, and the increase in
expenditures induced by a sea ferry service. The effect on development would
be determined partly by the amount of additional expenditures generated and the
multiplier effect on income and employment. In order for the effect to be pervasive,
there would have to be a continuing and expanding flow of island residents and

tourists to other islands. There are many indications that out-of-state visitors are going to go in increasing numbers to the neighbor islands. If a ferry system in turn leads to a much greater movement of local residents, the combined effect of both increased out-of-state visitor and local resident travel would give much greater momentum to development.

Therefore, the key aspects on development would be the induced travel by local residents with cars for vacations and other trips, the length of stay by visitors at each of the islands, and the amount and type of expenditures. This is not to disregard increased travel by out-of-state visitors and a lengthening of the periods of stay at the other island. Experience conclusively shows that a flow of tourists generates investments and encourages "supporting" businesses such as hotels, motels, restaurants, gas stations, retail stores, all kinds of service establishments, and even small scale industry. A good example of the economic impact of a ferry system through encouraging tourism is the Alaska Ferry System. According to a recent study based on its first year of operation, the Alaska ferry system has encouraged substantial investments in tourist accommodations and related activities such as gas stations, automobile repair services, retail stores, and restaurants.[2] Along these lines a Hawaiian ferry should encourage some movement of labor, capital, and enterprise and expansion of permanent population in the neighbor islands.

However, all our analysis in this report is based on the assumption that a ferry will give people a comfortable trip, will be convenient for people with automobiles, will be efficiently operated, and will be accepted by local residents and out-of-state visitors as a means of transport. Even assuming these important factors, we do not believe that a ferry system would induce increasing numbers of

[2] See Wolf Management Services, Investment Opportunities in Southeastern Alaska, Technical Assistant Project, Area Redevelopment Administration, U. S. Department of Commerce.

local residents to travel to the other islands year after year as we pointed out earlier, unless the state takes positive steps before the system goes into operation, to improve key highways, develop and improve recreational facilities, and build cabins. The roads to some of the major attractions on the neighbor islands have deteriorated, and in some cases are practically impassable; there are no roads to some of the loveliest beaches, recreational areas, and scenic attractions. Furthermore, in order to have a repeated and increasing flow of visitors to the neighbor islands, there would have to be private investments in medium and lower-priced hotels, motels, restaurants and many other types of businesses that serve tourists. We presume that such investments would take place.

In other words, a ferry system cannot be an effective carrier of economic development unless the State government makes complementary economic and social overhead investments. If the state decides to establish a ferry system, it should be conceived as a part of a system to foster development. This system would consist of highway construction, improvement of seaports, development of recreational facilities and cabins, improved education, more effective aid to farmers and small industry, and other activities to speed development.

3. Redistribution of Income from Oahu to the Neighbor Islands

A point of view that we have heard during the course of our study is that economic activity generated by a ferry system might involve some transfer of income from Oahu to the neighbor islands. From our survey of households and other available information, there is no question that Oahu residents would do most of the travel to the other islands. To some extent, especially in the case of induced travel, this would involve a shift of expenditures from Oahu to the other islands. The increased expenditures could in turn stimulate more economic growth on the neighbor islands. On the other hand, there would be some return movement of residents from the neighbor

islands to Oahu. According to our estimates, about 80 per cent of passenger traffic island residents would be from Oahu to the neighbor islands and the rest would be from the neighbor islands to Oahu.

Table VIII-2 shows an estimate of the possible shift in expenditures and personal income from Oahu to the neighbor island, that might be generated by a new ferry system in the first year of its operation. The estimates in this table are based largely on data developed in Chapter VII, Section 1 and previous chapters. According to these estimates there would be an increase in expenditures of about 9 million dollars and an increase in personal income of about 9.2 million dollars on the neighbor islands during the first year as a result of the ferry operation. On the other hand, there would be an insignificant reduction in expenditures and personal income of less than a half million dollars on Oahu.

The increase in personal income on the neighbor islands would have some impact on their economic growth, but the shift from Oahu would have negligible adverse consequences on the growth of the island. The growth impact on the neighbor islands would be considerably greater when we consider the expenditures on harbor and terminal facilities, and the public overhead expenditures cn highways, cabins, and supporting facilities, which may have to be undertaken as part of the entire system.

Of greater consequence would be the private investments in hotels, motels, restaurants, and other facilities that would be induced by the increased flow of residents and out-of-state visitors to the neighbor islands. When the business investments induced by the ferry system are considered, the impact of a ferry system on personal income in the neighbor islands would be substantially greater. While limited data is available, it seems quite reasonable to assume that the induced investments would about equal the increased visitors expenditures during the initial period of investment expansion lasting about two or three years.

191

TABLE VIII-2

ESTIMATE OF REDISTRIBUTION OF PERSONAL INCOME
BETWEEN OAHU AND THE NEIGHBOR ISLANDS
FIRST YEAR OF A FERRY OPERATION
(Thousands of Dollars)

	Oahu[1]	Neighbor Islands[1]	Total State
Changes in Expenditures			
Induced tourists			
31,000 tourists spending $44 for an average stay, half involving a reduction of expenditures on Oahu	(680)	1,360	680
Diverted tourists			
31,000 tourists spending $13 more as a result of saving in transportation costs	--	403	403
Diverted residents			
110,000 travelers spending $15 more because of savings in transportation costs	330	1,320	1,650
Induced residents			
51,500 households spending an average of $20 per day for an average stay of 7.7 days	[2]	5,923	5,923
Total Changes in Expenditures	(350)	9,006	8,656
Multiplier effect on personal income (Change in expenditures x 1,023)	(358)	9,213	8,855

[1] The estimates in this table on changes in expenditures by residents are based upon 80 per cent of the travel by Oahu residents to the neighbor islands and 20 per cent by residents of neighbor islands to Oahu.

[2] The shift of expenditures of Oahu residents to the neighbor islands estimated at about $1.4 million is offset by the expenditures of neighbor island residents on Oahu.

Note: Totals may not add because of rounding.

192

Under this assumption considering the multiplier, a ferry system would expand personal income on the neighbor islands by an estimated 18.5 million dollars during the first year of its operation. The induced private investments on the neighbor islands should not be considered as a shift from Oahu, but rather an increase in total investments in the state.

From a more comprehensive point of view, the development of neighbor islands encouraged by a ferry system should not be looked at as a redistribution of income from Oahu to the neighbor islands. Such developments would not be at the expense of Oahu. The island of Oahu will largely benefit from such development, since it is a major supplier of goods, services and capital to the other islands. As an example, when terminal and harbor facilities are constructed on the neighbor islands, some of the expenditures will be made for materials and services provided by Oahu companies. Moreover, business firms in Oahu will share in the growing demand for goods and services as more people travel to the other islands. An Oahu businessman can be expected to make some of the increased investments on the neighbor islands. In summary, a ferry system could encourage a somewhat more rapid growth in the neighbor islands than in Oahu or what might be termed some "catching-up." To the extent that this happens, there would be feedbacks that would increase demand for goods and services produced or distributed by Oahu businesses and also increase opportunities for private investments.

4. Some Limitations of Development Induced by a Ferry System

We do not want to overemphasize the economic development impact of an inter-island ferry system. Tourism has limitations as a leading sector in economic growth. In itself it is a narrow basis for growth. While tourism has probably been a leading sector in the recent rapid growth of Oahu, it has not been alone. Oahu has had a considerable wider economic base because it has been Hawaii's

center of military and federal government expenditures, the pineapple and sugar industries, diversified manufacturing, banking, finance, domestic and external commerce, shipping, communications, and diversified agriculture. It is also a highly urbanized area. Therefore, we do not foresee that tourism induced by a ferry system would stimulate the kind of development on the other islands that has taken place on Oahu.

Another aspect is that tourism and supporting activities do not stimulate the effective development of an economy. Tourists are not a substitute for a permanent population. We do foresee some increase in permanent population, if tourism and supporting businesses are considerably generated by a ferry system. Still much of the market would still be the demand of local and out-of-state visitors, who stay for limited periods of time. Tourist industries do not stimulate economic growth as much as many types of manufacturing, commerce, finance and complementary activities do. They are not characterized by the internal and external economies and rapidly rising productivity. The kinds of jobs developed in tourist establishments such as hotels and restaurants are usually low paying. Also, the business and employment generated by tourism is likely to have seasonal peaks and declines. While a considerable increase in tourism would tend to encourage somewhat greater urbanization, the neighbor islands would presumably continue to be predominantly rural in character. As long as the neighbor islands continue to be primarily agricultural and rural, their development is likely to be limited.

What the increased travel of island residents and out-of-state visitors to the neighbor islands could do is to serve as a leading sector to ignite other types of development. In conjunction with complementary public investments of an economic and social overhead type and private investments, this could encourage structural changes in the production and marketing of diversified agricultural

products, development of more local industries, a breaking down of some vicious circles that hold back development, and an increase in the permanent population. The combination of these mutually-reinforcing developments could lead to more rapid economic growth of the neighbor islands.

From the discussion, it is clear that the establishment of an inter-island ferry system is not a panacea for the development of the neighbor islands. There are other alternative programs to foster greater economic growth in the other islands, including more concentration on the production and marketing problems of diversified agriculture and the development of local industries. Nevertheless, to the extent that a ferry system would bring large numbers of people to the neighbor islands, it would create momentum that could spur development of other key sectors of the economy.

5. Non-Economic Aspects

Sometimes, the non-economic aspects of a new transportation system have the most far reaching consequences. The researchers in this study do not have any special competence in this area; but they feel it is appropriate to make a few broad comments because of the importance of the non-economic factors. An inter-island sea ferry system by providing an alternative, less expensive method of transportation could link the major islands more closely together politically, socially, and culturally. It could help to overcome some of the feeling of remoteness, and isolation of the people on the neighbor islands. It could contribute to making the state a more cohesive political unit. One of the barriers to closer political and social cohesion of the Hawaiian islands may be the isolation of the people on the neighbor island. The greater movement of people among the major islands would do a great deal to overcome this isolation. Even more effective would be a considerable expansion of population on the neighbor islands and more urbanization. A ferry system could contribute to such developments.

CHAPTER IX

AN ECONOMIC MODEL: REVENUES, COSTS
AND ECONOMIC IMPACT OF THE PROPOSED FERRY, 1970-1974

In this chapter, we shall build an economic model for 1970-1974, the five years following the first year of ferry operations.

In Chapter II, p. 52, we pointed out that projections of time series beyond 1969, the first year of ferry operations, have no empirical basis. However, for reasons already explained we present here an economic model in order to illustrate the analytical process which could have been made if such empirical information were available. In fact, this is a sample of what could have been done if funds and time were available for the use of a computer. In such a case, the present analytical process could have been applied to different sets of assumptions.

Our model is based upon very specific assumptions. Needless to say, its results will be meaningful only if the assumptions upon which the model is built hold true.

1. General Assumptions

This model is based upon assumptions we have emphasized previously and in this chapter.

a. The ferry system will provide passengers with a comfortable trip and efficient service. As a result, it will attain public acceptance.

b. With public acceptance, there will be modest and fairly steady growth in passenger travel by ferry. This will include tourists as well as island residents.

c. There will be repeated travel on the ferry by island residents for vacations, pleasure, and for business purposes.

d. Operating and administrative costs will be kept under tight and effective control. Labor unions will be reasonable with respect to crew requirements, wages, other benefits, and other aspects of employment.

2. Revenues and Operating Costs

If we assume that the operating costs of the proposed ferry except the fixed debt service charges will increase after 1969 at a compound rate of 3.3 per cent per annum, then we are able to project estimates for such costs for the period 1970-1974. The 3.3 per cent rate is obtained by taking the average rate of increase of mid-point cost estimates from 1965 to 1969. (See Table IX-1.) At this growth rate, the lower, mid-point, and upper estimated operating costs of the proposed ferry for 1970-1974 may be projected as shown in Table IX-2.

TABLE IX-1

COMPUTATION OF RATE OF INCREASE OF OPERATING COSTS
EXCEPT DEBT SERVICE CHARGES, 1965-1969
(Thousands of Dollars)

	1965	1969	Per Cent Per Annum
Low estimate	$2,831[1/]	$3,212	3.1%
Mid-point	3,174	3,615	3.3%
High estimate	3,517[2/]	4,018	3.4%

[1/] Including $19,000 or $24,000 ÷ 1.24 representing loss of revenue to the ferry due to repairing of ships if the ferry is in operation in 1965. This figure was not included in Table IV-5 on the ground that there is no ferry operation in 1965. However, for computing compound rate of increase, it must be included. The figure 1.24 is the growth factor for revenues between 1965 and 1969 at 5.5 per cent per annum, the derivation of which is given in Table IX-3.

[2/] Including $58,000 or $72,000 ÷ 1.24. The reasoning in footnote 1 also applies here.

Sources: Tables IV-5 and IV-6.

L. Revenues and Operating Costs

If we assume that the operating costs of the proposed ferry except the fixed debt service charge will increase after 1964 at a compound rate of 3.5 per cent per annum, then we are able to project estimates for such costs for the period 1970-1974. The 3.5 per cent rate is obtained by taking the average rate of increase of mid-point cost estimates from 1965 to 1969. (See Table IX-1.) At this growth rate, the lower, mid-point, and upper estimated operating costs of the proposed ferry for 1970-1974 may be projected as shown in Table IX-2.

TABLE IX-1

COMPUTATION OF RATE OF INCREASE OF OPERATING COSTS
EXCEPT DEBT SERVICE CHARGES, 1965-1969
(Thousands of Dollars)

	1965	1969	Per Cent Per Annum
Low estimate	$2,974	$3,214	2.1%
Mid-point	3,143	3,611	3.5%
High estimate	3,512	4,018	3.4%

1/ Including $19,000 or $24,000 f $1.24 representing loss of revenue due to ferrys due to repairing of ships if the ferry was in operation in 1965. This figure was not included in Table IX-1. In the ground plant there is no ferry operation in 1965. However, in computing the compound rate of increase, it must be included. The figure is 2% in the growth factor for revenues between 1965 and 1969 at 3.4 per cent per annum, the derivation of which is given in Table IX-1.

2/ Including $52,000 or $47,000 f $2.2% the reasoning in footnote 1 also applies here.

Source: Tables IV-3 and XX-2.

197

TABLE IX-2

PROJECTED OPERATING COSTS OF THE PROPOSED FERRY, 1969-1974
(Thousands of Dollars)

	Lower			Mid-Point			Upper		
Year	Debt Service Charges	Other Operating Costs[1]	Total	Debt Service Charges	Other Operating Costs[1]	Total	Debt Service Charges	Other Operating Costs[1]	Total
1969	$900	$3,212	$4,112	$1,172	$3,615	$4,787	$1,443	$4,017	$5,460
1970	900	3,318	4,218	1,172	3,734	4,906	1,443	4,150	5,593
1971	900	3,428	4,328	1,172	3,857	5,029	1,443	4,287	5,730
1972	900	3,541	4,441	1,172	3,984	5,156	1,443	4,428	5,871
1973	900	3,658	4,558	1,172	4,115	5,287	1,443	4,574	6,017
1974	900	3,778	4,678	1,172	4,251	5,423	1,443	4,725	6,168

[1] Projected at a rate of increase of 3.3 per cent per annum.

Source: Tables IV-5 and IV-6.

198

In a similar manner, we shall assume that revenues of the proposed ferry will increase after 1969 at a compound rate of 3.4 per cent per annum and make projections for 1970-1974. This rate is derived by using the mid-point revenues of 1965 and 1969, and assuming that, with only one exception, revenues from induced traffic will increase after 1969 at the same rate as they were expected to increase between 1965 and 1969, while revenues from diverted traffic will not change at all. The exception is that we assume by 1974 there will be some cargo traffic induced by the ferry which will be equal to 30 per cent of the diverted cargo in 1969 (and also 1974, as we assume that the diverted cargo revenue remains constant). The computation of the 3.4 per cent is given in Table IX-3, and the projected revenue estimated are given in Table IX-4.

We may now combine the projected revenues and operating costs and observe possible profits and losses for 1970-1974. We shall combine the upper cost estimates with the lower revenue estimates in Table IX-5 as we did in Table V-5. As stated previously, the estimates must be interpreted in the light of numerous assumptions listed in this and the previous chapters.

3. Primary Net Ferry-Generated Expenditures

For estimating primary net ferry-generated expenditures for 1970-1974, and for computing the multiplier effect, we shall use only the mid-point estimates of traffic demand and costs.

We shall further assume that because of the economic activities generated by the ferry system, its initial adverse effect on existing inter-island carriers and car rental firms may be entirely offset in five years by an increase in their business due to overall expansion of the economy caused by the ferry. For the sake of simplicity, we shall subtract a flat 20 per cent every year until the adverse effect is reduced to zero in 1974. This is shown in Section I of Table IX-6 which contains operating costs of the ferry and cutbacks induced by ferry operations.

199

TABLE IX-3

COMPUTATION OF RATE OF INCREASE
OF REVENUES OF THE FERRY, 1965-1969
(Thousands of Dollars)

	1965	1969[1]	Per Cent Per Annum 1965-1969	1974[2]	Per Cent Per Annum 1974
Passenger revenues					
"Diverted" state residents	$1,154	$1,351	4	$1,351	0
"Induced" state residents	1,132	1,324	4	1,611	4
"Diverted" tourists	276	434.5	12	434.5	0
"Induced" tourists	276	434.5	12	766	12
Automobile revenues					
"Induced" passenger cars	$ 627[3]	$ 734	4	$ 893	4
"Diverted" passenger cars	135	170	6	170	0
"Diverted" commercial cars	253	319	6	319	0
"Induced" commercial cars	--	--	--	95.7[4]	--
	$3,853	$4,766	5.5	$5,640.2	3.4

[1] See Table V-4. For state residents, the ratio of "diverted" to "induced" is 50.5 - 49.5 while for tourists it is 50 - 50. For passenger cars $170,000 (which is 8,500 cars x 20) is subtracted from the total to get the "induced" passenger cars.

[2] Assuming that revenues from induced traffic increase as they were expected to do so between 1965 and 1969 while revenues from diverted traffic do not change.

[3] 734 ÷ 117 = 627 (growth at 4 per cent per annum).

[4] 30 per cent of diverted commercial cars.

200

TABLE IX-4

PROJECTED REVENUES OF THE PROPOSED FERRY, 1969-1974[1]
(Thousands of Dollars)

Year	Lower	Mid-Point	Upper
1969	$3,999	$4,766	$5,533
1970	4,135	4,928	5,721
1971	4,276	5,096	5,916
1972	4,421	5,269	6,117
1973	4,571	5,448	6,325
1974	4,726	5,633	6,540

[1] Projected at a rate of increase of 3.4 per cent per annum.

Source: Table V-5.

TABLE IX-5

PROJECTED REVENUES AND OPERATING COSTS OF THE PROPOSED FERRY, 1969-1974
(Thousands of Dollars)

		Upper-Lower	Mid-Point	Lower-Upper
1969:	Operating Costs	$5,460	$4,787	$4,112
	Revenues	3,999	4,766	5,533
	Profit (Loss)	($1,461)	($ 21)	$1,421
1970:	Operating Costs	$5,593	$4,906	$4,218
	Revenues	4,135	4,928	5,721
	Profit (Loss)	($1,458)	$ 22	$1,503
1971:	Operating Costs	$5,730	$5,029	$4,328
	Revenues	4,276	5,096	5,916
	Profit (Loss)	($1,454)	$ 67	$1,588
1972:	Operating Costs	$5,871	$5,156	$4,441
	Revenues	4,421	5,269	6,117
	Profit (Loss)	($1,450)	$ 113	$1,676
1973:	Operating Costs	$6,017	$5,287	$4,558
	Revenues	4,571	5,448	6,325
	Profit (Loss)	($1,446)	$ 161	$1,767
1974:	Operating Costs	$6,168	$5,423	$4,678
	Revenues	4,726	5,633	6,540
	Profit (Loss)	($1,442)	$ 210	$1,862

Source: Tables IX-2 and IX-4.

202

TABLE IX-6

PRIMARY NET FERRY-GENERATED EXPENDITURES, 1969-1974
(Millions of Dollars)

		1969	1970	1971	1972	1973	1974
I.	**Operating Costs of Ferry and Ferry-induced Cutbacks**						
a.	Operating Costs Other Than Debt Service Charges	$3.62	$3.73	$3.86	$3.98	$4.12	$4.25
b.	Cutbacks	4.83	3.86	2.90	1.93	0.97	0
	Total	($1.21)	($0.13)	$0.96	$2.05	$3.15	$4.25
II.	**Additional Consumption Expenditures**						
a.	"Induced" Tourists[1]	$0.63	$0.76	$0.85	$0.95	$1.06	$1.19
b.	"Diverted" Tourists	0.40	0.40	0.40	0.40	0.40	0.40
c.	"Diverted" State Residents	1.65	1.65	1.65	1.65	1.65	1.65
d.	"Induced" State Residents[2]	5.92	6.16	6.41	6.67	6.94	7.22
	Total	$8.65	$8.97	$9.31	$9.67	$10.05	$10.46

[1] The formula is $22 x 31,000 x (1 + 12\%)^t$ where t=1, 2, 3, 4, 5 for 1970, 1971, 1972, 1973 and 1974.

[2] $115 x 51,500 x (1 + 4\%)^t$. See footnote [1] for t.

203

We shall use the same assumptions with regard to additional consumption expenditures of people taking the ferry. Since we already have such expenditures computed for 1969 in Table VII-1, we need only to add the additional consumption expenditures to be spent by the "induced" state residents and tourists in later years. This is done in Section II of Table IX-6.

4. Multiplier Effect

We shall use the same multipliers as developed in Chapter VII, but add the assumption that there is a one-year lag in the multiplier effect. We shall not include induced investment in our model because it is such a complicated and shiftable economic activity that a simplified version will not do it justice while our time and budget will not allow us to investigate it fully. The general discussion we had in Chapter VIII on possible investments in the neighbor islands will apply equally here.

In addition, our analysis is confined to the possible net impact of the ferry on the state economy as a whole. The possible shifting of economic activity from Oahu to the neighbor islands is not included here.

The final results of our model are presented in Table IX-7 which is self-explanatory.

204

TABLE IX-7

MULTIPLIER EFFECT OF THE FERRY, 1969-1974
(Millions of Dollars)

	Primary Net Ferry-generated Expenditures		Increase in Gross Domestic Expenditures (Multiplier =1.733)	Increase in Gross Domestic Product (Multiplier =1.199)	Increase in State Personal Income (Multiplier =1.023)
	Construction of Terminal Facilities	Operating Costs, Cutbacks, and Additional Consumption			
1967-1968	$3.80	--	--	--	--
1969	--	7.44	6.59	4.56	3.89
1970	--	8.84	12.89	8.92	7.61
1971	---	10.27	15.32	10.60	9.04
1972	--	11.72	17.80	12.31	10.51
1973	--	13.20	20.31	14.05	11.99
1974	--	14.71	22.88	15.83	13.50
1975	--	--	25.49	17.64	15.05

Source: Tables VII-4 and IX-6.

TABLE IX-7

MULTIPLIER EFFECT OF THE FERRY, 1965-1974
(Millions of Dollars)

	Primary Ferry-Generated Expenditures		Increase in Gross Domestic Product (multiplier =1.333)	Increase in Gross Domestic Product (multiplier =1.199)	Increase in State Personal Income (multiplier =1.025)
	Construction of Terminal Facilities	Operating Costs, Cutbacks, and Additional Construction			
1947-1968	$3.80	--	--	--	--
1969	--	7.44	6.35	2.56	3.89
1970	--	8.84	11.59	8.92	7.61
1971	--	10.27	15.32	10.60	9.04
1972	--	11.72	17.80	12.31	10.51
1973	--	13.20	20.31	14.05	11.99
1974	--	14.71	22.88	15.83	13.30
1975	--	--	23.49	17.64	15.05

Source: Tables VIII-5 and IX-6.